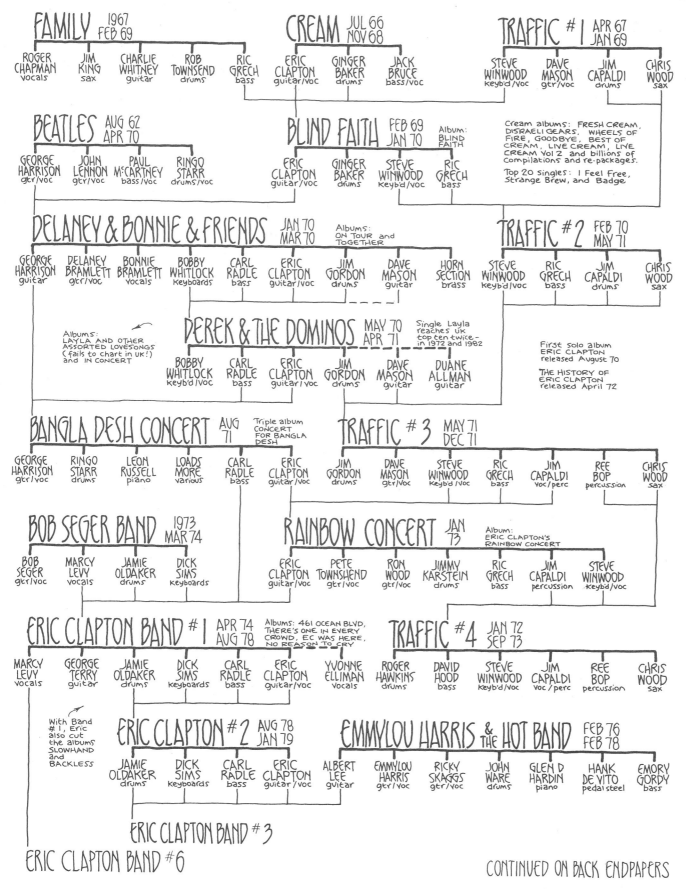

CONTINUED ON BACK ENDPAPERS

Slowhand

·THE LIFE & MUSIC OF ERIC CLAPTON·

Slowhand

·THE LIFE & MUSIC OF ERIC CLAPTON·

MARC ROBERTY

HARMONY BOOKS

New York

ACKNOWLEDGEMENTS

*Marc Roberty would like to thank the following people for their help and
encouragement: Bill Levenson at Polyram New York as well as Denis M. Drake and
all his team down at Polygram's Tape Facility in Edison, New Jersey, who tolerated
an amazing amount of noise as I went to and from the tape library; Christina
Basciano for her help in editing some of my ideas and her understanding of lap top
computers; Joe McMichael for his incredible diligence in researching obscure USA
tour dates; Virginia Lohle for her large collection of photos; Jo and Susie at Harvey
Goldsmith's for always looking after me; Alphi and Sally O'Leary for also
looking after me; and John Peck for his photos.*

*I would also like to thank the following people for their tolerance and friendship over
the years: Mady and Guy Roberty, Pat McDonald, Rose Clap, Heather Sorensen,
Karen Daws, Bob and Maryanne Mortimore, David and Kirsti Hill, Roger Forrester
and last but not least, the ever helpful Di!*

PHOTOGRAPHIC ACKNOWLEDGEMENTS
The Publishers wish to thank the following photographers and organisations for their kind permission to reproduce their photographs in this publication: Camera Press/Alex Agor 84, 86/Chris Horler 95b/ Snowdon 54t; Deran Records (Decca Record Company Ltd) 23; Jean-Pierre Leloir half-title page, 34b, 76b, 89l, 108t; London Features International 6, 12–13, 16–17, 29, 31, 34t, 44b, 50, 65, 70, 71l, 72–3, 76t, 82, 83b, 90, 92, 93, 108–9, 144, 157t, 161b, 164tl; Tom McGuiness 8–9; Pictorial Press 16, 18, 26–7, 74tl/Star File 30b, 33, 36, 44t, 73b, 80b/David Seelig 141b; David Redfern 28, 32t, 68–9, 72b, 163b, 166t; Redferns/ Richard Aaran 100–1; Relay 32b, 52, 85, 152b/ Andre Csillag 110/Chris Walter 88; Repfoto/Robert Ellis 75t, 79b, 103, 135/Rick Fuscia 117/Barrie Wentzell 35b, 39, 58, 66–67, 71r, 78t, 78b; Rex Features Ltd 42–3, 91b, 132, 139, 167tl, 168r/ Bellisimo, LGI 161t/Camera 5 45/Dezo Hoffman 79t/Silver Clef Enterprises Ltd 1990 130–1, Debra Trebitz 113; Marc Roberty 134r, 147t, 150b, 153b, 155b/C Basciano 154l, 158b/John Peck 158t; Scope Features 89t/ Allan Ballard 89br/ Albert Ferreira, DMI 140, 156b/Transworld 146/ Kevin Winter, DMI 124; Star File 123b, 147b, 166tr/Richard E Aaran 111, 122/Mickey Adair 120–1/Lydia Criss 119/Jim Cummings 50–1/Andre Csillig 48–9/Dagmar 59l, 75b/Oliver Dziggel 107t/ Bob Gruen 77l, 81b, 112, 118t, 167tr/Mike Guastella 168l/Mark Harlan 105/Larry Kaplan 106/Elliot Landy 56–7, 59r, 60t/Bob Leafe 115/ Joel Levy 159b, 164b/Virginia Lohle 91t, 153t, 155t/Tom Lucas 46/Jeffrey Mayer title spread, 77r, 87, 134t, 167b/Paul Natkin 94, 95t, 142/Philip Ollerenshaw 160, 163t, 164tr/Anastasia Pantsios 107l/Chuck Pulin 121, 123t, 136, 156t, 165, 166tl/David Seelig 141t, 151/Andy Seghers 159t/ Gene Shaw 137, 152t/Joe Sia 54b, 62–3, 64, 81t, 83t, 108b/Steve Weitzman 45/Barrie Wentzell 35t, 37, 38t, 38b, 53, 60b, 74/Vinnie Zuffante 114, 126, 149b, 150t, 157b; 154r; David Wedgbury, courtesy Deram Records (The Decca Record Company) 20–1; Val Wilmer 30t.

Published by Harmony Books, a division of Crown Publishers Inc.,
225 Park Avenue South, New York, New York 10003

Originally published in 1991 in Great Britain by The Octopus Publishing Group
part of Reed International Books Limited, Michelin House, 81 Fulham Road, London SW3 6RB

HARMONY and colophon are trademarks of Crown Publishers Inc.

Printed in Great Britain

ISBN 0-517-58351-8

10 9 8 7 6 5 4 3 2 1

First Edition

Library of Congress Cataloging-in-Publication Data:

Roberty Marc
    Slowhand: the life and music of Eric Clapton/by Marc Roberty.
      p.   cm.
    Includes discography and index.
    ISBN 0-517-58351-8: $30.00:
    1. Clapton, Eric. 2. Rock musicians--Biography. I. Title.
ML419.C58R63 1991
788.87'166'092--dc20   91-7602
  [B]   CIP

CONTENTS

Introduction

I was first aware of Eric Clapton's guitar playing back in the mid Sixties when I mistakenly played the flip side of the Yardbirds' 'For Your Love' single. The number was 'Got To Hurry', and featured an amazing solo that was like nothing I'd heard before. I never played the 'A' side again. It also led me to research as much information on this guitar player as possible.

I've followed Eric's musical exploits ever since and, equally important, sought out his influences. I would recommend anyone who wants a better understanding of his music to do the same – it will take you on an amazing journey through sounds and styles, starting with the blues of Robert Johnson, Muddy Waters and Chuck Berry through to reggae, country and other influences as diverse as Bob Marley, Don Williams and The Band.

I first met Eric through a mutual friend in the early Seventies and found him to be a kind and generous man, though troubled at the time. I got to know him a lot better in the Eighties, meeting at various parties and concerts. It was then I decided to launch *Slowhand*, the official Eric Clapton magazine which I also edited, with the full approval of Eric and his manager Roger Forrester.

Lengthy interviews with both Eric and fellow musician Gary Brooker for *Slowhand* formed a basis for researching this work, and Roger Forrester's office proved more than helpful in providing valuable data covering tour dates and such.

My research took me to Polygram, New York where special Projects Director Bill Levinson enabled me to visit their tape facility in Edison, New Jersey, where most of Eric's tapes from his RSO days are kept. With the help of Director Dennis Drake I was able to go through the tape boxes and labels, the hand-written comments from producers and engineers at the sessions being particularly revealing. I was also fortunate enough to hear a lot of unreleased tracks from the Cream days through to 1980.

Likewise, American Clapton enthusiast Joe McMichael undertook exhaustive research across the US which involved him talking to promoters and agents, and spending literally hours on end scouring local libraries for much of the press material reproduced here.

During a lifetime of record collecting and concert-going I have also built up a personal collection of Clapton information and memorabilia, which has provided both the inspiration and backbone of this book.

MARC ROBERTY, 1991

Eric Clapton with the guitar
that bears his name, the
charcoal grey 'EC Signature'
Stratocaster

EARLY DAYS

*E*ric Clapton's early history was archetypal of the generation of young musicians who forged the British rock revolution in the 'Sixties..

Born in the leafy suburbs of southern England, he attended the local grammar school before becoming an art student. At the time, art school meant much more than just another college; it was a catalyst for a distinct stream in late Fifties teenage sub-culture, a new bohemianism involving beards, beat poetry, ban-the-bomb, and — as often as not — blues.

An underground cult, black American blues attracted a nucleus of fanatical followers who were zealous in defending and promoting their taste; purist certainly, but therefore utterly dedicated. It was this evangelical dedication that drove Eric to master his chosen art, the blues guitar.

And things were changing swiftly. Blues was moving out of the back rooms of pubs to college dances and clubs; when he first heard the rivetting electric R&B of Alexis Korner, the sweat-soaked sound of Chicago right there in London's West End, Eric knew that music was going to be his life.

Eric Clapton's very first band, the Roosters, with (left to right) Clapton, Robin Mason on drums, vocalist Terry Brennan, Tom McGuinness on bass

SCHOOLTIME

Eric Patrick Clapton
Born Ripley, Surrey, UK
March 30th 1945

E ric Patrick Clapton had wanted to be a musician from the age of six, when he played recorder in the school band at Ripley Church of England Primary School.

Born on 30 March 1945, he grew up in the quiet Surrey village in the care of his grandmother, Rose Clapton and her second husband Jack Clap. Eric's surname came from Rose's first husband, his mother's father, Reginald Clapton. When Eric was born his mother, Pat, was just 16 and unmarried, while his father — a soldier called Edward Fryer — returned to his native Canada and wife. Pat then moved to Germany with another Canadian serviceman, Frank McDonald, leaving Eric with her parents.

The little school band gave Eric an immediate buzz, and an ambition to play an instrument started there. He had fantasies of being a trumpeter or a drummer. Like all kids of his generation, he was brought up on the radio — the wireless. On programmes like the Sunday lunchtime 'Family Favourites' and Saturday morning 'Children's Favourites', among the classical, nursery and novelty records rare nuggets of blues-tinged pop and jazz could be found, with artists such as Johnnie Ray and Earl Bostic. By the time he was 13, Fats Domino and Elvis Presley were sandwiched between 'Pomp and Circumstance', 'The Runaway Train' and 'Laughing Policeman'.

By the mid 1950s, Clapton was in his early teens and, fuelled by the sounds of Elvis Presley, Bill Haley, Chuck Berry and Buddy Holly, he burned to be a musician. And as he was later to recall, the natural way the blues and rock'n'roll musicians played really didn't look that difficult. He managed to persuade his grandparents to buy him an acoustic guitar, a Spanish Hoya, that cost fourteen pounds in Bell's Music Shop, Surbiton.

Schoolwork began to suffer as he slavishly copied his guitar heroes, a roster that by now included bluesmen like Big Bill Broonzy and Brownie McGhee who had received international exposure — even the BBC Light Programme! He would sit at the top of the stairs at home, to get an approximation of an 'echo' effect, and practise by ear, instruction manuals proving of no use or interest.

Despite the guitar getting in the way of his studies at Hollyfield Road School in Surbiton, he managed to pass his A-level exam in his best subject, art. This, along with his portfolio of work, won him a place at Kingston College of Art in 1959.

Art schools at that time were hothouses of creativity in various fields, and as soon as Clapton started the course he fell in with a crowd who shared similar musical tastes. Socially, this extended to the Kingston beatnik musical scene based in the Crown pub. Here he could play with people of like mind, and initially superior ability. He hung around the Crown, and the L'Auberge coffee bar in nearby Richmond, and eventually beatnik haunts in London's West End that centred on the Duke of York pub in Rathbone Place, just north of Oxford Street.

Neglect of his studies in stained glass design led to his expulsion from college in 1962, but although he was initially disappointed, he saw it as a chance to devote more time to the guitar. While working on a building site by day, he became more involved in the London beatnik lifestyle, spending more and more time at the blues club on Eel Pie Island. Eventually he gave up his casual labour, and often slept on park benches or crashed out on people's floors.

Clapton soon discovered the world of the West End jazz clubs, which themselves were undergoing something of a transformation at the time. The British jazz scene was a hotbed of puritanism — whether 'traditional' jazz purists who championed the revival of New Orleans jazz, or the 'mods', modernists who scorned anything more dated than the early 1940s bebop of Charlie Parker. The clubs were similarly identified with these stylistic camps; Ronnie Scott's in Gerard Street was a 'modern' venue, so too was the Flamingo just down the road on Wardour Street. Ken Colyer's Studio 51 in Great Newport Street was a hive of trad purism, as was Cy Laurie's place in Ham Yard. Only the Marquee, headquarters of the National Jazz Federation and then located under the Academy Cinema in Oxford Street, operated a catholic policy of trad one night, modern another, big band another; and from mid-1962 it began featuring Thursday night Rhythm and Blues sessions with Alexis Korner's Blues Incorporated.

Korner was a catalyst for the burgeoning R&B

scene. His own band featured, among others, Graham Bond, Dick Heckstall-Smith, Ginger Baker and Jack Bruce — new young players from the modern jazz community who nevertheless wanted to bridge the gap that had developed between sophisticated jazz and its roots in the blues. The interval spots at the Marquee sessions were usually filled by a group of teenage players, based in the Ealing Blues Club (which Eric frequented), Keith Richards, Brian Jones and a London School of Economics student named Mick Jagger.

Inspired by this time by the electric blues of Muddy Waters, Jimmy Reed and the 'Chicago' sound exemplified by Korner and the Ealing bunch, Eric Clapton realized his next step had to be to acquire an electric instrument. Again with financial help from his grandparents, he bought a double cutaway Kay, the model he had seen Korner playing.

Clapton began playing around the Kingston and Richmond folk pubs with another folk-blues guitarist, Dave Brock; around at the same time was another folk-blues duo, featuring Roger Pearce and an ex-artschool associate of Eric's, Keith Relf. Clapton began hanging out with the three Ealing players he had seen doing the Marquee intervals, who by January 1963 had got themselves a drummer, Charlie Watts, who had played with Alexis Korner occasionally, and Bill Wyman on bass. They'd even decided on a name, culled from a Muddy Waters song, the Rollin' (without the 'g') Stones.

THE ROOSTERS

Early in 1963, a girl who had been at Kingston Art College with Eric introduced him to her boyfriend, Tom McGuinness, who was looking for a guitarist for a group he was forming with Ben Palmer on piano, Robin Mason on drums and Terry Brennan handling most of the vocals. A kindred blues purist, Palmer was a great influence on Clapton. They called the band the Roosters, presumably after the Willie Dixon song 'Little Red Rooster'. They rehearsed at the Prince of Wales pub in New Malden and played around the south west London suburbs wherever they could find

a gig. Most of their bookings were at private parties with the odd 'commercial' date, usually the Ricky Tick clubs in Kingston, Windsor or West Wickham.

Although devoted to the blues, Clapton was eager to explore the rock'n'roll end of R&B, the music of Chuck Berry and Bo Diddley, while Palmer really wanted to stick to the straight and narrow of Chicago blues. This divergence ended up in the Roosters' disbanding after six months, though as much through lack of outside interest as in internal disagreements.

Tom McGuinness, meanwhile, had heard that a Liverpool group, Casey Jones and the Engineers, were looking for a couple of guitar players. He and Eric got the job, and spent an unlikely couple of months on the northern beat circuit. Casey Jones was Brian Casser, a seminal name in Liverpool beat mythology as Cass of the legendary Cass and the Casanovas. Although the initial glamour of driving up north for gigs made the two London-based men feel they were exploring new territory, they were breaking no new ground musically. Casey's ambitions were straight pop with a single view to the big time. He had hustled himself a one-record deal with the Columbia label, and the single was made with Casey plus session men, but he needed a band on the road. Clapton left after a handful of gigs playing material totally inappropriate to his taste, soon followed by an equally disenchanted McGuinness.

■ T O U R S ■

EARLY LIVE APPEARANCES
Autumn/Winter 1962
With guitarist Dave Brock, various folk pubs and clubs around Kingston/Richmond area of Surrey, including the Crown, Kingston and L'Auberge coffee bar, Richmond.
Early 1963–Autumn 1963
With Roosters, various gigs around Surrey area to south and west of London, including the Ricky Tick clubs in Windsor, Kingston and West Wickham, and the Wooden Bridge Hotel Guildford.
Late 1963
Six weeks with Casey Jones and the Engineers, based in Liverpool and playing Northern beat and cabaret circuit.

FIVE LIVE YARDBIRDS

*A*long with the Animals from Newcastle and Birmingham's Spencer Davis Group, the Yardbirds were in the front line of the army of R&B groups storming the country and the charts in 1964 in the wake of the Rolling Stones' forays the previous year.

British blues, based on the music of Muddy Waters and Jimmy Reed, Chuck Berry and Bo Diddley, was enjoying an unprecedented boom, spearheaded by precociously talented young players like Stevie Winwood, Brian Jones and Eric Clapton.

The Yardbirds had a definite sound of their own, a high-energy, blistering approach based on a frantic rhythm section that was anchored by the sheer dynamic of Clapton's stunning phrasing on lead.

But almost-overnight success saw them pitched into the deep end of the pop business, hectic one-nighter tours interrupted only by pressure from management and record company to make more and more commercially successful singles.

It was pressure Eric, still a purist at heart, could do without. Yet the initiation into the high profile world of pop that the Yardbirds provided was to stand Eric in good stead at subsequent stages of his career.

*The Yardbirds. Rear: Chris
Dreja, Jim McCarty, Paul
Samwell-Smith. Front: Eric
Clapton and Keith Relf*

BLUESWAILIN'

First recordings
R. G. Studios, London
October 1963

By mid-1963 the Rolling Stones were enjoying a highly successful residency at the Richmond Crawdaddy Club, in the Station Hotel. The Liverpool-led beat boom was in full swing, and now the Stones were being tipped as London's answer with their raw brand of R&B. At the end of September the Stones, whose debut single had made it No. 21 in the charts, were on the road in a UK package tour headlined by the Everly Brothers and Bo Diddley. Their residency at the Crawdaddy had been taken over by a local group, the Yardbirds.

Keith Relf, frontman vocalist with the group, had known Clapton at art school and he and the rest of the band had seen him around the Kingston pubs. After returning from the Liverpool fiasco, Clapton went to the Crawdaddy to check them out. The band's line-up then was Relf on vocals and harp, Chris Dreja on guitar, Jim McCarty on drums, Paul Samwell-Smith on bass and Anthony Topham on lead guitar. Topham was finding it hard to resist parental pressure to devote more time to his academic studies, and was about to leave the group; Eric was offered his place, which he accepted without hesitation. So in October 1963 Clapton became a Yardbird.

The Yardbirds had the same dedicated attitude to the blues as the Roosters, but were a little more adventurous in terms of new material. Contemporary R&B by the likes of Bo Diddley and Jimmy Reed, usually unavailable on the British market, was continually trawled to add to their repertoire.

Eric Clapton moved into a top floor flat in Kew with Keith Relf and Chris Dreja, enjoying once again the bohemian existence which seemed highly appropriate to a working musician. The Yardbirds were not exactly overburdened with work initially, just the

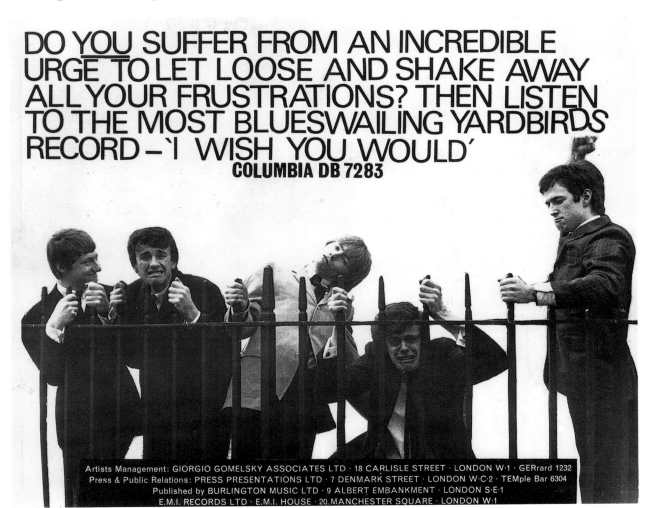

Typically zany Sixties group shot – Eric's on the right in this advert for the Yardbird's debut single

Crawdaddy residency and a regular spot at the Studio 51 in London's Soho. That was until the Crawdaddy promoter, a Russian-Swiss by the name of Giorgio Gomelsky who had briefly managed the Stones, became interested in the group. Gomelsky signed the band to a management contract, and Eric with his grandmother Rose (who had to sign as well, he being under 21) duly committed himself at Keith Relf's house with the other families of the teenage Yardbirds. Working with Gomelsky was Hamish Grimes, a young graphic designer, who took over the group's image with such inspired advertising slogans as 'The fabulous blues-wailing Yardbirds'.

That same month of October that Eric had been recruited, Gomelsky had helped promote the American Blues Festival package at the Fairfield Hall, Croydon. The overall European tour was organized by a German impressario and record producer, Horst Lippmann, and featured top blues artists including Muddy Waters, Memphis Slim, Willie Dixon and Sonny Boy Williamson. Williamson stayed on for his own tour of Britain and after some initial concerts with Chris Barber's Jazz Band he used the Yardbirds as his regular backing group. For Clapton, a blues fan but a relative newcomer to professional playing, it was a case of being thrown in at the deep end. Williamson could be difficult to say the least; he would change the numbers round without warning, lurch mid-tune into another song, hang back on some lines, leave others out. But this baptism of fire was one that Eric and the other Yardbirds wouldn't have missed for the world. There was also a live album recorded at the Crawdaddy by Lippmann in December 1963 but not released until 1966.

■ TYPICAL CLUB SET ■

Autumn 1964

Yardbirds Beat • Boom Boom • I'm A Man • I Ain't Got You • A Certain Girl • Slow Walk • Who Do You Love • Can't Judge A Book • Got Love If You Want It • Louise • Here 'tis • Pretty Girl • Respectable • Too Much Monkey Business • Good Morning Little Schoolgirl

Gomelsky was nevertheless determined they should be part of the current recording boom in R&B bands, and booked them into the R.G. Jones studios in Morden, Surrey, to record some demos which he hawked round to the two major record companies, Decca and EMI. They eventually signed to EMI in February 1964, cutting three tracks almost immediately.

The Yardbirds had already secured a Friday night residency at the Marquee in January (rhythm and blues, a club-based cult that was becoming a nationwide fashion, was now clearly taking precedence over jazz at this venue), and in addition to this, the Crawdaddy and a weekly gig at the Star in Croydon, they were begining to work up and down the country. The Sonny Boy gigs had given the band immediate kudos among the swelling ranks of R&B fans, and now they had their first taste of one-night stands nationwide, in their own right rather than as a backing group.

BOOMTIME

When their first single, 'I Wish You Would' (a cover of a number by Billy Boy Arnold) came out in June 1964 the Yardbirds had clocked up thousands of miles in a gruelling schedule that took them from civic halls in Scotland to blues pubs in Cornwall, now-legendary venues like the Manchester Twisted Wheel to seminal centres of R&B such as the Newcastle Go-Go club and the Cavern, Liverpool.

During that hectic six months of touring they made their first album, a live Marquee session recorded in March 1964. Other highlights punctuating the endless succession of truck-drivers' cafes, seedy hotels and sweaty clubs and ballrooms, included appearing on the first British Rhythm and Blues Festival at Birmingham Town Hall in February. But for Clapton, this was all eclipsed by his first session work as a guest guitarist, on an album recorded in London with Muddy Waters, Muddy's pianist Otis Spann, Ransome Knowling on bass and Little Willie Smith on drums. It was a dream come true, and Eric played on two tracks, 'Pretty Girls Everywhere' and

'Stirs Me Up'. The sessions were produced by blues enthusiast and entrepreneur Mike Vernon, and engineered by Roy Baker and Gus Dudgeon. Vernon, with his brother Richard, went on to found Blue Horizon, an important label in the second British blues boom in the late 1960s, while Baker and Dudgeon both became prominent record producers. This was Clapton's first proper meeting with his hero Muddy Waters, and the two remained very much in touch in a warm relationship that lasted until Muddy's death in 1983.

After their frenetic touring schedule plugging the single night after night, the Yardbirds' manager decided the boys deserved a break. However, what they imagined was going to be a holiday in Gomelsky's home town of Lugano, Switzerland, turned out to be an engagement to play every night at the side of the hotel swimming pool! This was just one example of 'informal' business done in the Yardbirds' name but without their prior agreement. Clapton felt, as their reputation grew, that artistically too things were slipping away from their direct control.

On their return the band played the Fourth National Jazz and Blues Festival at Richmond on 9 August. Keith Relf, who suffered from frequent bouts of asthma, had been hopitalized with a collapsed lung.

Eric with his Mod look of short hair, Ivy League Jacket, tab-collar shirt and 'slim Jim' tie

Mick O'Neill took over on vocals, and at the end of their set they were joined for a jam by Georgie Fame, Graham Bond, Ginger Baker and Mike Vernon. This was not the first time Relf's condition meant his absence, and sets being reduced to 'jams' to supplement the gaps in repertoire.

One memorable all-nighter at the Twisted Wheel in Manchester had John Mayall, still based partly in Manchester in 1964 and an inveterate 'sitter-in' on blues harp, jamming on a twenty-minute blues with the Yardbirds minus Relf and members of the Liverpool support band the Clayton Squares. Similarily, a session at the Crawdaddy saw Rolling Stone Brian Jones sitting in on harp.

◼︎ *At the height of their pop fame on TV's 'Ready Steady Go', the guitars are still going through tiny Vox AC30 amplifiers*

POPSTAR

▬▬▬▬▬▬▬ **T**his was a far cry from their next move into the pop mainstream. To promote their second single 'Good Morning Little Schoolgirl' in September 1964 the Yardbirds were put on a big package tour headlined by Billy J. Kramer, Cliff Bennett and the Nashville Teens. The tour, which finished mid-October, was followed quickly by a second trek in an equally mixed bag of a line-up that included Jerry Lee Lewis and one-hit-wonder Twinkle!

These packages required the group to play three or four numbers, including their current single of course; on stage and off in a matter of minutes.

In December their live tracks at the Marquee were released as the album *Five Live Yardbirds*. More than any studio album could have done, it captured the dynamism and atmosphere of the Yardbirds' often frantic stage act; it was also where Giorgio Gomelsky, in the album sleevenotes, first coined the nickname 'Slowhand' for Clapton.

Later that month they were the opening act on the Beatles' Christmas concerts at London's Hammersmith Odeon. Although they were bottom of the bill, the Yardbirds almost stole the show with a loyal 'home crowd' turning up every night. Eric Clapton actually designed the Yardbirds' suits on the Beatles show. They reflected his 'mod' inclination at the time, an Ivy League look that flew in the face of the current fashion to follow the style of the Fab Four from Liverpool. While Eric persisted in a short-cropped mod haircut, the rest of the group were happy to sport the 'mop top' look still *de rigeur* among pop groups. This was another symptom of the slide into commercialism which Clapton tried harder and harder to resist.

His dissension began to be noticeable soon after the Christmas shows. He took a few days' holiday with his mother and stepfather at their home in Germany, Relf's old pub partner Roger Pearce standing in. When he returned in the New Year, Clapton noticed the group had been quite relieved not to have him round, as his criticism and concern at the way things were going got more prevalent, against the grain of the rest of the group's thinking.

He felt that 'Good Morning Little Schoolgirl' was about as far as they could go in terms of commercial pop singles while still retaining a genuinely R&B feel. His increasing unease that the band was losing — or at least changing – its direction, came to a head around the issue of the third single. They could not agree on a number for the single, so Gomelsky told them all to go off and think about it and see what they could come up with, bearing in mind the aim was to be as commercial as possible with a view to a huge chart hit. Clapton's suggestion was an Otis Redding title, 'Your One And Only Man'.

Paul Samwell-Smith, meanwhile, had been appointed spokesman for the group by Gomelsky — a situation that seemed to undermine the positions of lead guitarist Eric Clapton and vocalist Keith Relf. Samwell-Smith had a number that had been submitted by songwriter Graham Gouldman: 'For Your Love'. It was obviously more catchy and commercial than Clapton's choice and the rest of the group went for it. That the single reached No. 3 soon after its release in March 1965 served only to increase the commercial pressure on the band. Eric hated the song with its harpsichord and bongo-drum backing, more so when he had to try to reproduce it on a 12-string guitar on stage every night. Ironically, the B-side of 'For Your Love', 'Got To Hurry', which featured some stinging guitar work, was the first song Clapton ever wrote, although credited to a Gomelsky non-de-plume, Rasoutin.

The single proved to be the crunch, and when a memo went round from the management for all ideas to be submitted through Paul Samwell-Smith, Clapton made it plain he didn't like it. He was called to Gomelsky's office and told that if he was unhappy, he could go. He agreed.

Happy-go-lucky group photographs didn't show up the many strains and frictions that came from a life of continuous one-nighters

DISCOGRAPHY

SINGLES:

I Wish You Would (*Billy Boy Arnold*)/
A Certain Girl (*Neville*)
U.K. Columbia DB7283/U.S.
Epic BN9709
Olympic Studios, London,
November 1963
Prod. Giorgio Gomelsky
Released July 1964

Good Morning Little Schoolgirl
(*Level, Love*)/
I Ain't Got You (*Carter*)
U.K. Columbia DB7391/No U.S.
release
Olympic Studios, London, March
1964
Prod. Giorgio Gomelsky
Released October 1964

For Your Love (*Gouldman*)/
Got To Hurry (*Rasoutin*)
U.K. Columbia DB7499/U.S.
Epic BN9790
IBC Studios, London,
Decemeber 1964 (A-side)
Olympic Studios, London,
November 1964 (B-side)
Prod. Giorgio Gomelsky
Released February 1965

ALBUMS:

FIVE LIVE YARDBIRDS
Too Much Monkey Business
(*Berry*), **I Got Love If You Want
It** (*Moore*), **Smokestack Lightnin'**
(*Burnett*), **Good Mornin' Little
Schoolgirl** (*Level, Love*),
Respectable (*Isley Bros*), **Five
Long Years** (*Boyd*), **Pretty Girl**
(*McDaniel*), **Louise** (*Hooker*), **I'm
A Man** (*Pomus, Shuman*),

Here 'Tis (*McDaniel*)
U.K. Columbia SX1677/No U.S.
release
Live recording, Marquee Club,
London March 1964
Prod. Giorgio Gomelsky
Released January 1965

**SONNY BOY WILLIAMSON AND
THE YARDBIRDS**
Bye Bye Bird (*Williamson,
Dixon*), **Mr Downchild**
(*Williamson*), **23 Hours Too Long**
(*Williamson*), **Out Of The Water
Coast** (*Williamson*), **Baby Don't
Worry** (*Williamson*), **Pontiac
Blues** (*Williamson*), **Take It Easy
Baby** (*Williamson*), **I Don't Care
No More** (*Williamson*), **Do The
Weston** (*Williamson*)
U.K. Fontana TL5277/U.S.

TOURS

1963
October
Weekly residency, Crawdaddy
club, Richmond
Weekly residency, Studio 51,
London
Various local bookings around
west London
November–December
Residencies at Crawdaddy and
Studio 51 continue. Touring
nationwide with Sonny Boy
Williamson

1964
January
Friday night residency at
Marquee, London
Weekly residency Star,Croydon
Crawdaddy residency continues
Touring one-nighters R&B circuit
February
One-nighters continue
February
28th First British Rhythm and
Blues Festival, Birmingham
Town Hall
March–July
One-nighters
July
Hotel engagement, Lugano,

Switzerland
August
9th 4th National Jazz and Blues
Festival, Richmond
September
Package Tour: Billy J. Kramer
and the Dakotas, Cliff Bennett
and the Rebel Rousers, Nashville
Teens etc.
September
18th Granada, Walthamstow
19th Colston Hall, Bristol **20th**
Odeon, Lewisham **21st** Granada,
Maidstone **22nd** Granada,
Greenford **23rd** Gaumont,
Ipswich **24th** Odeon, Southend
25th ABC, Northampton **26th**
Granada, Mansfield **27th** Empire,
Liverpool **28th** Caird Hall,
Dundee **29th** ABC, Edinburgh
30th Odeon, Glasgow
October
1st ABC, Dublin **2nd** Adelphi,
Belfast **3rd** Savoy, Cork **4th** ABC,
Stockton **7th** ABC, Carlisle **8th**
Odeon, Bolton **9th** Granada,
Grantham **10th** ABC, Hull **11th**
Granada, East Ham **13th**
Granada, Bedford **14th** Granada,
Brixton **15th** Odeon, Guildford
16th ABC, Southampton **17th**
ABC, Gloucester **18th** Granada,

Tooting
November
Package Tour: Jerry Lee Lewis,
Twinkle etc.
6th Hippodrome, Brighton
**December 24 1964–January 16
1965**
'Another Beatles Christmas
Show', Hammersmith Odeon,
London: The Beatles, Freddie
and the Dreamers, Elkie Brooks,
Jimmy Saville, Sounds
Incorporated etc.

1965
February–March
One-nighters

BLUES BREAKER

*T*he Bluesbreakers enabled Eric to take his blues crusading onto a technically superior plane. John Mayall was a kindred spirit when it came to belief in the music, gathering around him the very best players in the field. And by 1965, that meant Eric Clapton.

The year or so with Mayall saw his playing mature from that of boy wonder to fully-fledged superhero of the electric guitar, his reputation achieving cult status as the legend 'Clapton Is God' identified his more fanatical followers.

When he became a Bluesbreaker his playing was considered merely brilliant, by the time he left he was rated among the best in the world.

Despite the band's considerable success, as their much-acclaimed LP climbed to No 6 in the charts Eric once again felt the need for a new musical challenge; but his time with Mayall represented, as captured on the album, the British blues boom at its' peak.

1965
April
John Mayall invites Eric
to join Bluesbreakers
June
Uxbridge Folk Festival
August
Leaves to form the
Glands
October
'I'm Your Witchdoctor',
recorded in summer,
released on Immediate
label
November
Rejoins Mayall after
abortive Greek
residency. Record
second single, 'Lonely
Years'. Session work on
album featuring
Champion Jack Dupree

1966
Spring
'Powerhouse', including
Bruce and Winwood,
recorded for Joe Boyd
March
Bluesbreakers record
album
June
Ginger Baker suggests
forming trio
July
Leaves Bluesbreakers as
album charts at No. 6

John Mayall, Eric Clapton,
John McVie and Hughie
Flint in an alternative
take to the one used on
the Bluesbreakers' LP
cover, later to appear on a
John Mayall compilation
album

ON THE ROAD AGAIN

*Clapton joins
John Mayall
April 1965*

The Yardbirds behind him, Eric Clapton decided to leave the London scene for a spell, in the wake of music press headlines that screamed 'CLAPTON QUITS YARDBIRDS — TOO COMMERCIAL'. He went to stay with his old friend Ben Palmer in Oxford, where he could lick his wounds and pour out his troubles about the Yardbirds' descent into the commercial mire.

Contrary to popular belief he didn't take the opportunity to practise all day, but he did try to persuade Ben into making a blues record together and travelling with him to Chicago. Whatever plans were being forged were forgotten, however, when he received a phone call from John Mayall asking him to join his band, the Bluesbreakers.

Born 12 years earlier than Clapton, Mayall hailed from Manchester where he had formed the Blues Syndicate in 1962 very much on the lines of Alexis Korner's Blues Incorporated. Korner persuaded him to chance his arm in London, where he moved in early 1963, though retaining a base in the north. After trying out many musicians, Mayall formed his first Bluesbreakers in the middle of that year and very soon became a respected voice on the growing R&B circuit.

Mayall had tracked Eric down to Ben Palmer's after reading about his departure from the Yardbirds in the *Melody Maker*. There was talk of an audition, but once Clapton returned to London he was in. The band featured Mayall on keyboards, harps and guitar, John McVie on bass, Hughie Flint on drums and Clapton lead guitar. At the same time Mayall let Eric move into his house, in London's Lee Green. He was given a tiny room of his own, where he was able to practise away from the family, and gradually explore Mayall's vast collection of blues records.

Apart from Ben Palmer, nobody seemed to have struck up a rapport with Clapton as Mayall did when it came to music. Here were two crusaders for the blues, for that in many ways was how they saw themselves, Mayall an emergent catalyst for those around him — again in the Korner tradition — and Clapton a fast-developing improviser of prodigious talent.

The Bluesbreakers, with Roger Dean on guitar, had already released two singles on Decca, plus a live album *John Mayall Plays John Mayall* recorded at the Klook's Kleek R&B club in the Railway Hotel, West Hampstead, London. Mayall was in complete command of his outfit. He demanded discipline from his players (he was substantially older than any of them) and got it. His dismissal of Roger Dean when Clapton became available was typical of his business-like but often perfunctory style.

Although the Bluesbreakers were solid, highly proficient players as individuals and a unit, it soon became apparent that Clapton's contribution was what more and more fans were turning up to see and hear. Yet the life of one-nighters to which he had now returned was still irksome. He loved the music, the vibes he created with his fellow players, the communication with an audience increasingly in awe of his talent — but life on the road was still a drag after a few months. Apart from the Uxbridge Blues and Folk Festival in the middle of June, on which they appeared with the Who, Long John Baldry, Spencer Davis and others, it was back to the bars, bandrooms and bed-and-breakfast that had characterized the Yardbirds' itinerary before their chart success.

Meanwhile, Clapton had encouraged Ben Palmer to move back to London to pursue his blues playing once more, while he himself shared a chaotic flat with two brothers, Jake and Ted Milton in London's Covent Garden, and it was during a heavy drinking session with Palmer, the Miltons and other cronies that the infamous Glands were conceived.

THE GLANDS

They came up with the mad idea of buying an old double decker bus in which to tour the world, playing the blues, stopping off at all the places they had always wanted to visit.

The drunken dream became surreal reality in August 1965 when Clapton announced he was leaving the Bluesbreakers, and set off in a huge American station wagon with Jake Milton, who played drums, Bernie Greenwood on sax, vocalist John Bailey, Bob Ray on bass and Ben Palmer on piano. They dubbed

Far left and left: *Tuning up and hanging round; studio work involves more pauses than actual playing, but the results of the Bluesbreakers sessions were a milestone in British blues*

themselves the Glands, and set off towards sunnier climes; first stop — Athens, Greece, hence their alternative name, the Greek Loon Band.

They got a job in a nightclub in Athens playing support to local headliners the Juniors. The whole gig was a disaster from the start. The club owner, a shady character surrounded by heavies yet obviously 'well in' with the local police, by some extraordinary oversight omitted to apply for work permits for the group and then used this as a lever when they protested at wages owed and hotel bills not paid. To worsen the situation, the Juniors had a road accident which left one dead and others seriously injured. The owner wanted Clapton to stay and play lead for the depleted Juniors — he wasn't going to lose his headline act — and so called in the police, on the work permit issue, to pressurize the other Glands into leaving without him.

The group decided to sell their equipment and use the proceeds to get Palmer and Clapton back to London and the rest of them on their way around the world. This became more difficult than they imagined. Planning to abscond from the gig with their equipment, they saw the plan thwarted when the management succeeded in locking Eric and his gear — including his prized Gibson Les Paul — in an upstairs

room as the others scrambled into their vehicle.

They sped to Athens to sell the equipment and plan Eric's escape, who had meanwhile convinced the owner he had to go and get his guitar restrung before he could do any further gigs. This enabled him to leave guitar in hand, minus his Marshall amplifier and most of his clothes. He was picked up by the others, who bought tickets for him and Palmer to travel back to London. As soon as they got off the train at Victoria Station, the first thing Clapton did was phone John Mayall, who welcomed him with open arms.

CLAPTON IS GOD

Mayall's reaction to the prodigal's return was not entirely magnanimous. Before his departure for the sun, Clapton was becoming the focal point of the band for more and more of its followers, many of whom stopped coming to gigs when he left. The slogan 'Clapton Is God' was beginning to appear on tube station walls, fans' leather jackets and the toilets of every R&B club in the land. He was becoming the centre of a cult. Mayall was astute enough to realize that the fading fortunes of his band while Clapton indulged his wanderlust could now be reversed with the guitarist's return. And he was absolutely right.

Once again Mayall's hiring and firing style became apparent, as Clapton's replacement Peter Green was now asked to leave after only three days. The Bluesbreakers also had a new bass player, Alexis Korner veteran Jack Bruce, who had been sacked from the Graham Bond Organisation, mainly as a result of friction between him and their drummer, Ginger Baker.

Bruce stayed only a few weeks — he had joined in August during Eric's Greek odyssey — but he and Clapton were instantly aware of a chemistry between them when they played. He left for a better-paid job with the Manfred Mann group, and was replaced by John McVie, whom Mayall had sacked previously for being drunk.

On Clapton's return to the band in November 1965 the Bluesbreakers recorded their first single at Wessex Studios in London's Soho under the supervision of Mike Vernon. They recorded two tracks, 'Lonely Years' and 'Bernard Jenkins' which were released on Vernon's Purdah label the following year. The band were so fanatical in their devotion to Chicago-style blues that the session was deliberately set up to imitate the primitive sound characteristic of the mecca of electric blues. This was achieved by using a single microphone suspended from the ceiling which created the desired effect of rough immediacy.

This was the second Bluesbreakers record to involve Clapton, the first being 'I'm Your Witch-doctor' in a one-off deal with Immediate Records released just a couple of weeks earlier. That was produced by Yardbird-to-be Jimmy Page. Through the Mike Vernon connection Clapton and Mayall also played on a session by American bluesman Champion Jack Dupree, who had taken up residence in northern England. Three tracks — 'Calcutta Blues', 'Shim Sham Shimmy' and 'Third Degree' appeared on Dupree's *New Orleans To Chicago* album.

With Eric's return, the Mayall band's following burgeoned once more. The 'God' references grew more numerous, to the point where it became outwardly an embarassment to Clapton in relation to the rest of the group, although privately he saw it as something of a vote of confidence in his own conviction and ambition — as one would.

Early in 1966, producer Joe Boyd was asked to put together a compilation of contemporary electric blues as a one-off project for the Elektra record company; to this end he wanted to get together the best British blues players for three tracks of the album. Unfortunately, most people he approached were signed to various labels with contracts that prevented them recording with anyone else, including John Mayall. Boyd enlisted the help of Manfred Mann vocalist Paul Jones, who managed after a week to get Eric Clapton on guitar, Jack Bruce on bass, and

the keyboards and drums from the Spencer Davis Group, Stevie Winwood and Pete York. Ginger Baker had been asked to fill the drumstool originally, but was either unavailable or quite likely reluctant to work again with Bruce, with whom he had constant disagreements in the Graham Bond band. Clapton and Joe Boyd spent a day listening to various blues albums choosing which numbers to record; eventually it came down to 'I Want To Know', 'Steppin' Out' and the Robert Johnson classic 'Crossroads'.

In March 1966 the Bluesbreakers recorded their first album at Decca's West Hampstead studios. Mayall, who had previously been with Decca, had now signed another deal with that label. The sessions managed to catch the band precisely at their peak; the album remains a milestone in British blues (most of which was not recorded for posterity at its best) and at the time confirmed the Bluesbreakers' growing stature, and that of Clapton in particular.

Billed as *John Mayall's Bluesbreakers featuring Eric Clapton*, the record underscored Eric's pre-eminence in the band, not just in his namecheck on the sleeve but on every track. His Les Paul played through a Marshall amp was recorded at stage volume as this was the only way to obtain the sustain and distortion required for his searing solos, and created a fair amount of technical difficulties for a studio in 1966. A seeming bonus at the time, but a portent of things to come, was Eric's first ever studio vocal on Robert Johnson's 'Ramblin' On My Mind'.

Jack Bruce rejoined the Bluesbreakers during April 1966 for a live album session at the Flamingo. Once again Eric was impressed with the musical rapport he achieved with the bass player, particularly on the band's regular material which inevitably got

■ TYPICAL SET ■

Spring 1966

Crossroads • I'm Your Witchdoctor • Have Your Heard • Parchman Farm • Stormy Monday • Double Crossing • Hideaway • Ramblin' On My Mind • Little Girl • Telephone Blues • Hoochie Coochie Man • Steppin' Out • What'd I Say

somewhat predictable when played night after night. Bruce injected a new dynamism into the proceedings which moved Clapton once again in the direction of change. He did nothing about it immediately, but early in May he was approached by Ginger Baker after a gig in Oxford, about the possibility of forming a group together. Eric reacted favourably to the idea, suggesting it could be just a trio, a virtuoso trio, comprising himself, Ginger and Jack Bruce on bass.

Baker's reluctance to get involved with Bruce was a legacy of their apparent feud while both were with Graham Bond, but Clapton still didn't realize the extent of the underlying emnity between them, and persuaded Baker to try and patch things up with Bruce to form this potential supergroup. This reconciliation was achieved after visiting Bruce, who was playing with the successful Manfred Mann but like Clapton felt the need for artistic change.

As the Bluesbreaker's album soared to No. 6 in the charts in July 1966, Eric Clapton announced he was leaving the band for the new trio which had already started rehearsing. John Mayall tried in vain to change his mind, and reluctantly accepted the guitarist's two week's notice. The new three-piece of Baker, Bruce and Clapton still didn't even have a name.

CELLAR CLUB
22a HIGH STREET, KINGSTON, SURREY
KIN 5856 / 6240

On WEDNESDAY, JUNE 3rd from America
THE GREAT
JOHN LEE HOOKER
with the
JOHN MAYALL BLUES BREAKERS
supported by the exciting new group
THE PLEBS
Admission: Members 7/6.   Non-members 10/-
Commencing 8 p.m.

■   D I S C O G R A P H Y   ■

SINGLES:
I'm Your Witchdoctor (Mayall)
Telephone Blues (Mayall)
UK Immediate IM 012
Recorded mid 1965
Prod. Jimmy Page
Released October 1965

▬

Lonely Years (Mayall)
Bernard Jenkins (Mayall)
UK Purdah 3502
Wessex Studios, London
November 1965
Prod.Mike Vernon
Released August 1966

▬

Parchman Farm (Allison)
Key To Love (Mayall)
UK Decca F12490
Decca Studios, London
March 1966
Prod. Mike Vernon
Released September 1966

ALBUM:
BLUES BREAKERS
All Your Love (Rush, Dixon)
Hideaway (King, Thompson)
Little Girl (Mayall) **Another Man**
(arr.Mayall) **Double Crossing**
(Mayall, Clapton) **What'd I Say**
(Charles) **Key To Love** (Mayall)
Parchman Farm (Allison) **Have
You Heard** (Mayall) **Ramblin'On
My Mind** (Johnson) **Steppin' Out**
(Frazier) **It Ain't Right** (Jacobs)
UK Decca SKL4804/US London
PS 492

Decca Studios, London
March 1966
Prod. Mike Vernon
Released July 1966

■   T O U R S   ■

▬

1965
April–August
The UK one-nighter circuit of colleges and R&B clubs, including the Marquee (London) Twisted Wheel (Manchester) Cavern (Liverpool) etc. Also the Blues and Folk Festival, Uxbridge,in mid June

▬

August-November
Athens, Greece (with the Glands)

▬

November 1965–July 1966
Continuous one-nighter circuit; Clapton's final gig with the Bluesbreakers was at the Marquee

THE CREAM YEARS

A relentless powerhouse of sound, Cream was the seminal supergroup that defined the dynamics of electric rock for the next decade.

Born out of the wailing blues of Clapton, the striding bass of Jack Bruce and roller coaster momentum of Ginger Baker's piledriver percussion, the collective musical energy took them way beyond the previous perimeters of rock music.

Fraught with internal tensions right from the start — tension that at times doubtless added to the musical sparks flying in all directions — the group neverthless were a bridge spanning the pop-based group scene of the first half of the Sixties and the exploratory 'progressive' rock that characterized the end of the decade; a link between the traditional blues-boom club circuit and mega-dollar stadium rock that had yet to come into its own.

For Eric Clapton himself, it was a milestone in his career that marked his personal transition from cult hero to superstar.

DIARY

1966
June
Starts rehearsing with Ginger Baker and Jack Bruce
July
Leaves John Mayall and formerly announces formation of Cream
July 29th
Debut appearance of Cream, the Twisted Wheel, Manchester
July 30th
National Jazz and Blues Fetival, Windsor
August 2nd
London debut, the Marquee
October
First single release, 'Wrapping Paper'
December
First album release, *Fresh Cream*

1967
January
'Fresh Cream' reaches No. 6 in album charts
April 3rd
U.S. debut, Murray the K's Fifth Dimension Show, New York
June
Fresh Cream starts 92-week run in U.S. album chart
August
Start of second U.S. tour, Fillmore Auditorium, San Francisco
December
Second album, *Disraeli Gears*, reaches No. 5 in U.K. and No. 4 in the U.S.

1968
Feb 29th
Start of longest-ever U.S. tour by British group
June 15th
Tour ends at Wallingford, Conn.
September
Announcement of Cream's disbandment
October 4th
Start of U.S. 'farewell' tour, Oakland Calif.
November 3rd
Last ever U.S. performance, Providence R.I.
November 26th
Cream's final appearance, Royal Albert Hall, London

STRANGE BREW

Previous page: *Ginger Baker, Jack Bruce and Eric in an early Cream publicity shot – flying jackets, bluejeans and Ginger's fur hat!*

Below: *The trio's initial down-to-earth image was a far cry from the Flower Power foppery of a year or so later*

Opposite: *Cream taking part in a late '66 edition of the legendary 'Ready Steady Go' British TV series which went out live every Friday evening*

Rehearsals for Eric Clapton's new project started in June 1966, after a post-gig meeting in the Prince of Wales pub, Guildford, following a Bluesbreakers show at the Plaza. Ginger Baker and Jack Bruce tacitly agreed to bury the hatchet, and the first get-together was arranged to take place in Ginger's house in Neasden. They toyed with the notion of calling the group Sweet'n'Sour Rock'n'Roll, but at that initial rehearsal Clapton commented that they were the 'cream' of the British blues scene, and Cream was the name eventually adopted.

Two years older than Eric, Jack Bruce had moved south to London in 1962 after studying at the Royal Scottish Academy of Music. Proficient on cello, bass and piano, he soon established himself playing bass on the London jazz and blues scene with groups like the John Birch Octet, Blues Incorporated and the Graham Bond Organisation. Similarily, Peter 'Ginger' Baker's background was in jazz, though initially 'trad' (dixieland) bands that included big names like Terry Lightfoot and Acker Bilk. His obsession with the drumming of English virtuoso Phil Seaman drew him into the world of modern jazz which, like Jack Bruce, he drifted away from in favour of the fledgling R&B scene.

Clapton's original concept was for Cream to be a modern blues outfit, with his country-blues background producing a potent foil to the jazz-blues playing of the rhythm section. He planned to do updated versions of songs written and recorded twenty or thirty years earlier by legendary names such as Robert Johnson and Son House. Baker and Bruce were fairly unfamiliar with much of this material, and heard most of it for the first time on records belonging to Clapton.

But even from the first rehearsal it was clear things were not going to be moulded by any preconceived plan. Jack Bruce arrived with some ready-written new songs and they became the basis of the new group's repertoire. Eric Clapton went along with it all because it was clear from the way things sounded at that first rehearsal that instrumentally the music was taking on a shape of its own. Jack's material included songs written in collaboration with the London poet Pete Brown, a partnership that would produce some of Cream's most successful numbers. Brown had been a seminal figure in the early 1960s, when under the banner of various poetry-and-jazz amalgams he brought together — as Alexis Korner later did in his more formal blues setting — such future instrumental luminaries as Stan Tracey, Graham Bond, Dick Heckstall-Smith, Jack Bruce and Ginger Baker.

Clapton's ambitions as lead vocalist took a back seat as well. Jack was already an experienced singer, having worked with Manfred Mann as well as the jazz/blues groups, and handled the songs with an assurance Clapton recognized he could not emulate without a lot of practice — practice they had no time for once the band was formally announced and about to go on the road. So by force of circumstance rather than pushing himself — in fact there was an element of reluctance in his taking on the role — Jack Bruce became the main vocalist in Cream.

DYNAMIC DEBUT

The band had an immediate offer of a management and recording deal from Robert Stigwood, who had already been involved with Baker and Bruce as manager of the Graham Bond group. So Cream's first concert was on 29 July 1966 at the Twisted Wheel, Manchester. They were driven up to the gig by Ben Palmer, who had been roped in by Clapton as a somewhat novice road manager, and already had an 'in crowd' cult following waiting for their debut despite a low-key build-up in the national music press.

The next day, however, things were rather different. Cream's second appearance was at the annual National Jazz and Blues Festival, held that year in Windsor, and a rain-soaked but expectant crowd of jazz/blues aficionados simply went bananas.

Right: Eric in action in December 1966 at the Roundhouse, one of the major London 'underground' rock venues of the period

Below: Another shot from a 'Ready Steady Go' TV show. Eric and Jack shared many of the vocals with Cream, though they gradually became a predominantly instrumental outfit

By the time they made their London debut, just three days later at the Marquee, their status was assured as both a 'musicians' group and a new rock phenomenon. In many ways the Marquee gig was the most crucial of their launch; the crowd at the outdoor Windsor event was carried along on a 'festival' atmosphere, the sound was less than perfect, so the more objective critics and music-biz opinion-makers were inclined to reserve judgement until the Wardour Street club gig. Musicians, eager to hear what the trio was up to, crowded the nearby Ship pub before the gig, where a restrained Jack Bruce sat with Pete Brown while Baker and Clapton fended off the press backstage at the Marquee club.

Recording had started almost immediately the group was formed with two tracks laid down at Chalk

■ SET LIST ■

The Marquee
2nd August 1966

Wrapping Paper • Cat's Squirrel •
Spoonful • Rollin' and Tumblin' •
I'm So Glad • I Feel Free

Farm Studios for Stigwood's Reaction label that would constitute the group's debut single: 'Wrapping Paper' backed with a reworking of an old blues, 'Cat's Squirrel'. The A-side, a fairly low-key Bruce and Brown song, was not released until October, by which time the trio had worked the club and college circuit extensively.

One memorable occasion on the long haul of one-nighters was on 12 October at Central London Poly-technic when Jimi Hendrix, newly-arrived in Britain, jammed with Cream. By the end of the year they had an album in the can, so while 'Wrapping Paper' was making just a minor dent in the lower reaches of the British Top 40, they were already plugging the follow-up 'I Feel Free' to be released in December 1966.

Some heavy promotion that included live radio sessions, television and even a trip to the trendy Locomotive Club in Paris in November, helped the single climb to No. 11 in the U.K. charts, followed in the L.P. lists by a No. 6 spot for their debut album *Fresh Cream*.

'I Feel Free' was an altogether more typical number from Cream than the debut single, and featured the then-revolutionary 'woman tone' which Clapton obtained by cutting out the bass control and turning up the treble and volume controls to maximum setting. *Fresh Cream* likewise was typical of the band's live set, including, along with originals, blues classics by Robert Johnson, Willie Dixon, Skip James and Muddy Waters.

AMERICA BECKONS

After a tour of France, Germany, Holland and Scandinavia early in 1967, the band took off for the U.S.A. to appear on Murray the K's Fifth Dimensional Show. Staged at the RKO Theater in New York, it involved twenty acts doing five shows a day. At the bottom of the bill,

Bruce, Baker and Clapton circa early 1967, as the band was poised to take America by storm

31

Eric's Marshall amp, seen behind him here, was twice the size of the old AC30s of the Yardbirds, but was nothing compared to the towering sound stacks to come

Cream were allotted just three minutes' playing time, in which they were able to squeeze one shortened number.

A bonus for Clapton on an otherwise unproductive trip was after the 10-day stint, when they were able to explore New York a little. They had been booked into Atlantic Studios to record some tracks for their second album, and during time off Eric began to get to know Greenwich Village. He met Al Kooper, at the time rehearsing the newly-formed Blood Sweat and Tears; he caught Frank Zappa several times, still an unknown quantity on the avant garde fringes of the rock scene. One night, at the Cafe A Go Go, he jammed on an incredible three hour set with B.B. King, the session being recorded by the management but never seeing the light of day either as an official release or as a bootleg.

The Atlantic sessions were produced by Felix Pappalardi; the engineer Tom Dowd was Atlantic's 'in house' veteran of a roster of stars ranging from Ray Charles to John Coltrane, and Clapton could hardly believe his luck to be in a studio working with technicians normally used to the company of people

As 1967 unfolded, Cream's horizons reached across the Atlantic with the prospect of conquering America

*Surrounded by psychedelia,
guitars and all, Ginger, Jack
and Eric during 1967's
Summer of Love*

Right: 'Shock headed' Eric, a far cry from the close-cropped Mod look of his days with the Yardbirds

Below: June 1967, and Cream prove they are the 'creme de la creme' with a concert at the Palais des Sports, Paris, France

like Aretha Franklin and Otis Redding. The entire album was recorded in the three days they had left before their work permits ran out.

SUMMER '67

On their return to England Cream found Jimi Hendrix had taken London by storm with his first album *Are You Experienced?* He was playing the main venues every night, and although by mid-summer they had been together over a year, they felt they were having to start from scratch to re-establish themselves on the British scene. To this end they again went through the promotional round of radio sessions, as many television shows as possible, and the Windsor Jazz and Blues Festival. They were more than taken aback therefore when manager Stigwood — who insisted their ultimate success lay across the Atlantic — turned down an to invitation appear at the Monterey Pop Festival. Hendrix, the Who and other heavyweight names were all doing Monterey, but Stigwood decided Cream should work in the U.S.A. in their own right.

He negotiated a series of concerts at Bill Graham's Fillmore Auditorium West in San Francisco followed by the Whiskey A Go Go in Los Angeles, the timing of which could not have been more fortunate. It was August in the legendary summer of '67, and the West Coast was in the grip of flower power and psychedelia. Cream's mind-blowing sounds provided the aural complement to the supposed chemical mind-expansion that audiences and musicians indulged in with apparent abandon.

Bill Graham allowed the band an 'open-ended' programme, meaning that they could extend numbers and improvise as they wished, which suited fans and band alike. Reviews were universally good; the influential *L.A. Free Press* remarked on the Whiskey shows that Cream were '. . . a truly ecstatic group of three from England. God bless England for her beautiful exports'.

Clapton was particularly impressed by the intensity of interest in music on the West Coast. His group shared the San Francisco bill with Paul Butterfield's Blues Band and the Electric Flag, two bands which he felt would never have been given a real chance in London. Compared to the highly competitive English pop scene, the laid-back idealism of the new American rock seemed to gel with his own 'purist' instinct that was naturally suspicious of commercialism. Ironically, as Cream moved east after the California gigs, they — and the whole West Coast 'progressive' rock scene — were becoming an increasingly commercial proposition. And of course the business interests that put them there in the first place, Stigwood, Atlantic Records and the rest, had banked on and indeed helped to engineer that situation from the start.

Starting at the Psychedelic Supermarket in Boston, Cream performed at Brandeis University,and the Greenwich Village Theater and Cafe A Go Go in New York, before spending a couple of weeks in Atlantic Studios laying down tracks for their third album, *Wheels Of Fire*. The highlight for Clapton came not when Cream were recording, but when a call from engineer Tom Dowd to his hotel invited

Eric, always a follower of fashion, was quick to adopt the tousled hair and gipsy look of the hippy era

Behind the ballyhoo: as life with Cream became more pressurized, Eric began to distance himself from the frictions developing in the trio

him to bring his guitar to the studio where a 'surprise' awaited. It turned out to be an Aretha Franklin session, for 'Good To Me As I Am To You', and although the Queen of Soul was not there in person, the musicians assembled for the backing track included some of the top studio players like Cornell Dupree, Joe South and Bobby Womack.

TOP GEARS

*T*hree nights at the Grandee Ballroom in Detroit brought their American trip to an end, and Cream returned to England at the end of October to begin plugging the release of their second album, *Disraeli Gears*. Beginning with a Brian Epstein-promoted concert at London's Saville Theatre on 29 October, the concert tour fell between two stools. With the summer success of their third single 'Strange Brew', which made No. 17 in the U.K. charts, they had some chart status as well as a burgeoning cult reputation; the nature of their music as well as their popularity made them too big for the club circuit, pop package tours were obviously inappropriate, and there was no developed circuit of stadium venues as in the United States. Nevertheless, *Disraeli Gears* proved to be their greatest success yet, reaching No. 5 in the British album charts and No. 4 in the U.S.A.

A short tour of Scandinavia at the end of 1967 came as a prelude to their longest trek across the United States, in fact it was the longest U.S. tour by any British band at that time, an almost continuous itinerary that stretched from late February 1968 into the middle of June. It came at a time when the old feud between Bruce and Baker, which had never really been resolved, was flaring more and more as

■ **SET LIST** ■
U.S. Tour 29th February–15th June 1968
Traintime • Steppin' Out • Crossroads •
Toad • Spoonful

life on the road got to each of the trio in various ways. Ultimately Clapton could not listen to the constant bickering between the other two any longer, and the three superstars even booked into separate hotels wherever possible.

Just as the band embarked on the marathon tour, 'Sunshine Of Your Love', a track taken from *Disraeli Gears*, became the band's first single to make the American Top 40 at No. 36. The strong showing in the album charts compared to the single says something about the way the rock audience, particularily the American rock audience, was moving at that time. It was the dawn of an album-oriented market that was to flourish in the late 1960s and redefine the audience for rock music in terms of the 'serious' music fan with a presumed greater spending power. And Cream, with their extended improvised solos normally associated with jazz records, was the first rock band whose music was genuinely more fitted to the album than single format.

GOODBYE

Despite rumours in the music press, Cream managed to present a facade of unity throughout the American tour. Soon after their return to England in mid-1968, the Stigwood Organisation made the announcement that after 'farewell' concerts in the U.S.A. and England, Clapton, Bruce and Baker would go their own ways. At the same time a double album, *Wheels Of Fire* was released, featuring tracks recorded in February at Atlantic Studios plus two sides of live material from their San Francisco dates in March.

During the three-month break the group enjoyed before the farewell tour kicked off in October, Clapton made what was to be his best-known contribution to someone else's record, when he played on George Harrison's song 'While My Guitar Gently Weeps' for the Beatles' *White* album. He had been a great friend of Harrison's since the Yardbirds' Christmas season with the Beatles at Hammersmith, and their lives continued to intertwine both professionally and privately through the next two decades.

A more incongruous project was Cream's sound-track music for the film *The Savage Seven*, which charted briefly on both sides of the Atlantic in the single 'Anyone For Tennis'. But a truer reflection of the band's popularity came in the sales of *Wheels Of Fire*, which became the group's biggest selling item yet. In the U.K. it was marketed as both a double album, which reached No. 3 in the chart, and as a single with just the studio tracks, which simultaneously made the No 7. slot. In the U.S.A. the album topped the charts for a month, and 'Sunshine Of Your Love'

Opposite: As the Sixties progressed, the style, like the music, got more flamboyant – and Cream were no exception

Below: Eric contemplates the future as the Cream years draw to a close

enjoyed a new lease of life, selling more than a million and making No. 5 in the singles chart.

So at the group's most successful point yet, a disbandment was now official. Euphoria surrounded the farewell gigs, particularly those at Madison Square Garden when the group were presented with platinum discs for *Wheels Of Fire*, and the emotional last-ever appearances at London's Albert Hall, and the trio were almost seduced into sticking together just to give it one more chance. But Clapton knew he was in need of new directions once again.

While in the United States for that final tour, he came across the Band through their *Music From Big Pink* album, and spent some time with them and Bob Dylan at their place in Woodstock, New York State. It was to have a profound effect on Clapton. He saw that the music of the Band and other contemporary American rock artists was drawn as much from a country/folk tradition as from the blues roots of his own playing. This opened up new vistas. Compared to what he felt was a strong lyrical quality in the Band's work that said something about their lives, Cream's own live performances had become exercises

Eric (right) and Cream (below) on stage together for the very last time at London's Royal Albert Hall, in what turned out to be an emotional farewell

Clapton collects the Melody Maker Pop Poll award for top International Musician in the Spring of '69, the applause afforded Cream worldwide still ringing in his ears

in technically spectacular self-indulgence.

The Albert Hall concerts, supported by Yes and Rory Gallagher's blues band Taste, were certainly charged with the affection that was apparent between the 10,000 fans, the thousands more outside, and the group. Cream had to explain to an almost pleading press why the band's music had developed as far as it could.

When they went into the studio the following week to record the *Goodbye* album, again things were so friendly, the atmosphere between the three of them so warm, that thoughts briefly strayed to a reunion; but it was clearly too late, and not to be. By the time *Goodbye* topped the U.K. album chart, in March 1969 (it was at No. 2 in the U.S.) Clapton had already taken the next step in his musical development. But a plethora of reissues, greatest hits albums and bootlegs, both at the time of their demise and over the years since, has demonstrated the affection and respect with which this band has been regarded. Cream was perhaps the most important milestone in Eric Clapton's career.

SINGLES:
Wrapping Paper *(Bruce, Brown)/*
Cat's Squirrel
(Trad.arr.S.Splurge)
U.K. Reaction 591007
Chalk Farm Studios, London
June, 1966
Prod. Robert Stigwood
Released October 1966

I Feel Free *(Bruce, Brown)/*
N.S.U. *(Bruce)*
UK Reaction 591011
Mayfair Sound, London
September 1966
Prod. Robert Stigwood
Released December 1966

Strange Brew *(Clapton, Collins, Pappalardi)/*
Tales Of Brave Ulysses *(Clapton, Sharp)*
U.K. Reaction 591015
Atlantic Studios, New York
April 1967
Prod. Felix Pappalardi
Released June 1967

Anyone For Tennis *(Clapton, Sharp)/*
Pressed Rat And Warthog *(Baker)*
UK Polydor 56258
Released May 1968

Sunshine Of Your Love *(Bruce, Brown, Clapton)/*
SWLABR *(Bruce, Brown)*
UK Polydor 56286/US Atco 6544
Atlantic Studios, New York April 1967
Prod. Felix Pappalardi
Released September 1968

White Room *(Bruce, Brown)/*
Those Were The Days *(Baker, Taylor)*
UK Polydor 56300/US Atco 6617
Atlantic Studios, New York
February 1968
Prod. Felix Pappalardi
Released January 1969

Badge *(Clapton, Harrison)/*
What A Bringdown *(Baker)*
UK Polydor 56315
I.B.C. Studios, London
December 1968
Prod. Felix Pappalardi
Released April 1969

ALBUM:
FRESH CREAM
N.S.U. *(Bruce)*, **Sleepy Time** *(Godfrey, Bruce)*, **Dreaming** *(Bruce)*, **Sweet Wine** *(Godfrey, Baker)*, **Spoonful** *(Dixon)*, **Cat's**

Squirrel *(Trad. arr. S. Splurge)*,
Four Until Late *(Johnson)*,
Rollin' and Tumblin' *(Waters)*,
I'm So Glad *(James)*, **Toad** *(Baker)*
UK Reaction 593001/US Atco SD 33-206
Mayfair Sound, London
September 1966
Prod. Robert Stigwood
Released December 1966

DISRAELI GEARS
Strange Brew *(Clapton, Collins, Pappalardi)*, **Sunshine Of Your Love** *(Bruce, Brown, Clapton)*, **World Of Pain** *(Collins, Pappalardi)*, **Dance The Night Away** *(Bruce, Brown)*, **Blue Condition** *(Baker)*, **Tales Of Brave Ulysses** *(Clapton, Sharp)*, **SWLABR** *(Bruce, Brown)*, **We're Going Wrong** *(Bruce)*, **Outside Woman Blues** *(Reynolds arr. Clapton)* **Take It Back** *(Bruce, Brown)*, **Mother's Lament** *(Trad. arr Cream)*
UK Reaction 593003/US Atco 33-232
Atlantic Studios, New York April 1967
Prod. Felix Pappalardi
Released November 1967

WHEELS OF FIRE
Record 1:
White Room *(Bruce, Brown)*, **Sitting On Top Of The World** *(Burnett)*, **Passing The Time** *(Baker, Taylor)*, **As You Said** *(Bruce, Brown)*, **Pressed Rat And Warthog** *(Baker, Taylor)*, **Politician** *(Bruce, Brown)*, **Those Were The Days** *(Baker, Taylor)*, **Born Under A Bad Sign** *(Jones, Bell)*, **Deserted Cities Of The Heart** *(Bruce, Brown)*
Record 2: recorded live:
Crossroads *(Johnson)*, **Spoonful** *(Dixon)*, **Traintime** *(Bruce)*, **Toad** *(Baker)*
U.K. Polydor 583031/2/U.S. Atco SD 2-700
Studio album only: UK Polydor 582033
Live album only: UK Polydor 582040

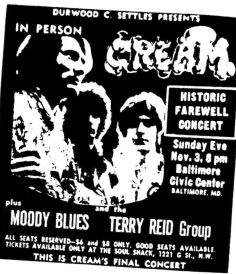

Record 1: Atlantic Studios, New York February 1968, except Track 1, IBC Studios, London August 1967 Record 2: Live at Fillmore West, San Francisco March 1968 *Prod. Felix Pappalardi* Released August 1968

GOODBYE
I'm So Glad *(James)*, **Politician** *(Bruce, Brown)*, **Sitting On Top Of The World** *(Burnett)*, **Badge** *(Clapton, Harrison)*, **Doing That Scrapyard Thing** *(Bruce, Brown)*, **What A Bringdown** *(Baker)*
UK Polydor 583053/US Atco SD7001
Tracks 1-3 live at the Forum, Los Angeles, October 1968
Tracks 4-6 IBC Studios, London December 1968
Prod. Felix Pappalardi
Released March 1969

LIVE CREAM VOL 1
N.S.U. *(Bruce)*, **Sleepy Time Time** *(Bruce, Godfrey)*, **Lawdy Mama** *(Trad. arr. Clapton)*, **Sweet Wine** *(Baker, Godfrey)*, **Rollin'and Tumblin'** *(Waters)*
UK Polydor 2383 016/U.S. Atco 33328
Recorded live, Winterland San Francisco 9–10 March 1968
Fillmore West, San Francisco 7 March 1968
Prod. Felix Pappalardi
'Lawdy Mama' prod. Robert Stigwood and Ahmet Ertegun
Released June 1970

LIVE CREAM VOL. 2
Deserted Cities Of The Heart *(Bruce, Brown)*, **White Room** *(Bruce, Brown)*, **Politician** *(Bruce, Brown)*, **Tales Of Brave Ulysses** *(Clapton, Sharp)*, **Sunshine Of Your Love** *(Bruce, Brown)*, **Hideaway** *(King, Thompson)*
U.K. Polydor 2383119/U.S. Atco 7005
Recorded live, Winterland San Francisco 8–10 March 1968
Forum, Los Angeles 19–20 October 1968
Prod. Felix Pappalardi
Released July 1972

TOURS

1966
July
29th Twisted Wheel, Manchester
30th National Jazz and Blues Festival, Windsor
August
2nd Marquee, London
August–November
UK club, ballroom and college circuit
November
19th Locomotive Club, Paris
November to February 1967
UK touring as above

1967
January
19th BBC Radio 'Saturday Club'
February
16th BBC Radio 'Saturday Club'
February–March
France, Holland, Germany, Scandinavia
March 25th–April 3rd
Murray the K's Fifth Dimensional Show, RKO Theater, New York
April
5th Radio show, Stockholm, Sweden
May-August
U.K. one-nighters
July
6th BBC Radio 'Saturday Club'
August
22nd–27th Fillmore Auditorium, San Francisco **29th–31st** Fillmore Auditorium, San Francisco
September
4th–6th Whiskey A Go Go, Los Angeles **7th** Psychedelic Supermarket, Boston
9th Brandeis University, Waltham Massachusetts
23th Village Theater, New York
26th Cafe A Go Go, New York
October
13th–15th Grandee Ballroom, Detroit
29th Saville Theatre, London
October–November
UK one-nighters
November
2nd BBC Radio 'Top Gear'
15th BBC Radio 'Top Gear'
November–December
Short tour of Scandinavia
December
BBC Radio 'Top Gear'

December–January
UK one-nighters

1968
Feburary 29th–March 2nd
Winterland, San Francisco
March
3rd Fillmore Auditorium, San Francisco
7th Fillmore Auditorium, San Francisco
8th–10th Winterland, San Francisco
March–April
Touring US
April
5th Back Bay Theater, Boston Brandeis University, Waltham, Mass.
May–June 15th
Touring U.S.A.
May
25th Civic Centre, San Jose, California
June
15th Oakdale Theater, Wallingford, Connecticut
October
4th Almeda County Collisseum, Oakland California **5th** University of New Mexico, Albuquerque **11th** New Haven arena, New Haven, Connecticut **12th** Olympia Stadium, Detroit **13th** Coliseum, Chicago **18th– 19th** Forum, Los Angeles **20th** Sports Arena, San Diego **24th** Coliseum, Houston **25th** Memorial Auditorium, Dallas **26th** Convention Centre, Miami **31st** Boston Garden, Boston
November
1st Spectrum, Philadelphia **2nd** Madison Sq. Garden, New York **3rd** Civic Center, Baltimore, **26th** Royal Albert Hall, London **4th** Rhode Island Auditorium Providence R.I.

BLIND
FAITH

*M*any would say that Blind Faith was doomed from the start, a victim of its own pre-ordained success.

After Cream, the idea of putting together a super-supergroup was ambitious to say the least. The trio of Baker, Bruce and Clapton had peaked commercially while at the same time pushing forward the musical frontiers of rock. To put together a completely new group but retaining two thirds of the old, Clapton and Baker, was asking a bit too much; the critics' forebodings were right, Cream Mark 2 was inevitable.

Winwood and Grech made their own contributions to the formula of course, but so great was the pressure for each star to perform their 'greatest hits', with Eric still the mega-hero of the bunch, that Blind Faith as an original creative unit never really had a chance.

Ginger Baker, Clapton and Stevie Windood during Blind Faith's Hyde Park debut concert, in front of 120,000 fans

SUPERGROUP

Debut concert
Hyde Park, London
June 7th 1969

Straight after the *Good-bye* sessions, it seemed time for Clapton to take it easy for a month or two. He was in the process of buying a house, Hurtwood Edge in Surrey, a 20-room mansion which was the main fruit of the success of Cream. While this was being finalized, his only professional activity was a couple of days at the Intertel television studios in Wembley just before Christmas 1968 filming the Rolling Stones' *Rock'N' Roll Circus*.

Like some other Stones projects around this time, the Circus idea seemed to echo what the Beatles had been up to a year or so earlier — in this case, the latter's *Magical Mystery Tour*, likewise a Christmas television special. Clapton was involved in a one-off group with John Lennon on rhythm guitar and vocals, Keith Richards on bass and Mitch Mitchell on drums. They played the Beatles' 'Yer Blues' and an

Far right: *Eric sits against a Fender Dual Showman amp and speaker, with his Gibson Firebird guitar*

Stevie Winwood, Rick Grech, Ginger Baker and Eric during rehearsals that took place at Eric's new home in Surrey

instrumental featuring improvised vocals from Yoko Ono; other stars in the show included the rest of the Stones, members of the Who, Taj Mahal and Jesse Ed Davies who Eric admired very much. Although it was finished on film, the whole project was aborted when the Stones decided their own contribution was below par, and has remained out of circulation except as a bootleg album and video.

While thinking about new musical ideas, Clapton followed through a notion he had formed during the last days of Cream, to add a keyboard to the line-up. His first choice for such a role was Stevie Winwood, in fact the two had discussed the possibility of some sort of collaboration. The time now seemed ripe, in that both musicians — Winwood had just wound down Traffic — were free of commitments. They rehearsed for weeks in Winwood's Berkshire cottage and Clapton's new house, and during February 1969 Ginger Baker arrived at the Winwood house offering his services as drummer. Winwood was very keen: he knew, as did Clapton, that Ginger was the best in the business, and particularly suited to what they had in mind. Clapton, naturally, was rather more cautious; he had sometimes bitter experience of Baker's fiery temperament, and was also apprehensive that the group might be dubbed 'Cream Mark II'.

Baker was taken on, however, and soon after that the rehearsals started to include preliminary recording sessions at London's Morgan Studios. The initial sessions mainly involved blues workouts, some Buddy Holly numbers and an assortment of songs worked out in their long hours of jamming at home.

Although a record deal had been agreed, the band — still without a name — was casting round for a bass player. They invited Rick Grech of Family to come on board, and he left his group in the middle of a U.S. tour to join them.

Polydor's publicity machine was already feeding the music press with anticipation of a new 'supergroup', which inspired Clapton's suggestion for a name, Blind Faith.

One diversion during the Blind Faith build-up was a film called *Supersession*, made in a studio in Staines, just outside London. Eric jammed with a strange collection of top musicians that included jazz saxophonist Roland Kirk, blues guitarists Buddy Guy and Buddy Miles, rock guitarist Steven Stills and British jazz/rock drummer Jon Hiseman.

The Hyde Park gig in June 1969; note Ginger Baker takes a front line position with the rest of the band, rather than the traditional 'backing' role of the drummer

BLIND ALLEY

Almost immediately Rick Grech joined Blind Faith, things accelerated. Although the musicians did not feel quite ready, their demo sessions at Morgan Studios suddenly became 'for real' album takes at Olympic, with producer Jimmy Miller at the control desk. While the album was still being mixed, Island Records put out an instrumental single taken from the Morgan sessions as a 'change of address' limited pressing for the trade. This in itself acted as a promotional hype for the forthcoming album.

Another event intended to whip up interest in this new musical phenomenon was a free concert announced to take place in London's Hyde Park on June 1969. In front of an estimated crowd of 120,000, Blind Faith's debut met with mixed reactions. Some people had expected them to sound like Traffic, while others hoped for another version of Cream. Of course they got neither, as the band performed numbers from the forthcoming album plus a version of the Stones' 'Under My Thumb' with a competent, though nervous, authority.

The band was clearly unprepared to debut at such a big event, and the next gigs, on a short tour of Scandinavia, were far more suitable. In contrast to the hype in England, it received very little promotion by the record company, and it was much more of a modest club circuit tour. Musically, the Scandinavian trek allowed them a lot more freedom to just blow, with Ginger Baker's 'Do What You Like' providing an extended solo spot for each musician in turn.

Eric looks apprehensive – with good cause – during Blind Faith's American debut at New York's Madison Square Garden

---

■ SET LIST ■
Hyde Park, London, 7th June 1969

Well All Right • Sea Of Joy • Sleeping In The Ground • Under My Thumb • Can't Find My Way Home • Do What You Like • In The Presence of The Lord • Means To An End • Had To Cry Today

---

Whatever Blind Faith might have developed into was abruptly brought to an end by their first and only American tour. Here the pressure was really on for them to reflect the audiences' expectation of another Traffic or Cream.

They opened at New York's Madison Square Garden on 12 July 1969 where they were greeted by a 15-minute standing ovation from the 20,000 fans before they had even played a note! They were not prepared for such a venue and lacked the necessary amplification to get their sound over; worse still, the revolving stage meant that what little sound they projected reached only part of the audience part of the time. By the final number the police had moved into the crowd to clear a way off stage for the group. This sparked off a 45-minute riot, and characterized much of the tour to follow.

The pressure to churn out the 'oldies' of their immediate past became irresistible as 20,000 fans a night were howling for their favourites from Traffic and Cream. For a band with only about an hour's worth of fresh material in their repertoire, it was an easy option — especially as the concerts, pitched in this way, were hitting the financial jackpot for promoters, record company and the players themselves.

As the American concerts became more and

more a 'business' proposition that the band dealt with as pure work, Clapton started hanging out with one of the support bands on the tour, Delaney and Bonnie, whose laid-back attitude was an antidote to the increasing tension in Blind Faith, particularly between himself and Ginger Baker. The heart was now almost visibly going out of the band.

Blind Faith's eponymous album was released in August 1969. It went gold and topped the charts on both sides of the Atlantic, while the U.S. tour got worse, with further violence between fans and police marring concerts, especially those in Los Angeles and Phoenix, Arizona. The group ended up having to trot out their old repertoire to appease the warring factions of teenagers and police.

Even the album's cover artwork was surrounded with controversy. Designed by an old friend of Eric's, Bob Ciderman, whom he'd met in San Francisco in 1967, it featured an 11-year-old girl, naked to the waist, holding a silver model airplane. A significant proportion of American dealers refused to stock the record in that cover, and a substitute was swiftly found by the record company, Atlantic.

After their last concert on the tour, in Honolulu at the end of August, Blind Faith simply drifted apart. Ginger Baker stayed on there with his family for a holiday, Rick Grech and Stevie Winwood went home while Eric Clapton went to Los Angeles where he stayed with Delaney and Bonnie and started planning a solo album.

DISCOGRAPHY

ALBUM:
BLIND FAITH
Had To Cry Today (*Winwood*), **Can't Find My Way Home** (*Winwood*), **Well All Right** (*Petty, Holly, Allison, Mauldin*), **Presence Of The Lord** (*Clapton*), **Sea Of Joy** (*Winwood*), **Do What You Like** (*Baker*)
UK Polydor 583059/US Atco SD 33-304
Morgan Studios, London Feb–March 1969
Olympic Studios, London May–June 1969
Prod. Jimmy Miller
Released August 1969

TOURS

1969
June
7th Hyde Park, London
12th Short tour of Scandinavia
July
North American tour
12th Madison Square Garden, New York **13th** Kennedy Centre, Bridgeport **16th** Spectrum, Philadelphia **18th** Varsity Stadium, Toronto **20th** Civic Centre, Baltimore **26th** County Stadium, Milwaukee **27th** International Amphitheater, Chicago

August
1st Olympia Stadium, Detroit **3th** Keil Stadium, St Louis **8th** Seattle Center Coliseum, Seattle **9th** PNE Coliseum, Vancouver **10th** Memorial Coliseum, Portland **14th** Almeda County Coliseum, Oakland **15th** The Forum, Los Angeles **16th** Arena, Santa Barbara **19th** Sam Houston Coliseum, **20th** Hemisfair Arena, San Antonio **22nd** Salt Palace, Salt Lake City **23rd** Memorial Coliseum, Phoenix **24th** Hic Arena, Honolulu

'...WITH ERIC CLAPTON'

*A*fter the traumas of superstardom, and the responsibility shouldered as the instrumental focal point of both Cream and Blind Faith (and the Bluesbreakers and Yardbirds before that) it was understandable that Eric should look for the relative anonimity of an accompanist's role for a change.

Like an extension of the various recording sessions by other stars that he participated on, the Plastic Ono Band really was a 'sitting in' gig that only lasted through two live appearances and one album. Nevertheless, with the goodtime rock'n'roll of Lennon and spontaneous anarchy of Yoko Ono, it showcased Eric's capacity for free-wheeling jamming as well as being of undoubted therapeutic value at the time.

The stint with Delaney and Bonnie was approached by Clapton in the same spirit, but by the end of one tour he felt his presence was being used to hype the band as a permanent unit. The lay-off from being mainman was over, heralding Eric, for the first time, fronting a band of his own.

DIARY

—

1969
September
Delaney & Bonnie
recording, A&M
Studios, Hollywood
September 13th
Toronto Rock'n'Roll
Revival festival
September 25–28th,
October 3–6th
'Cold Turkey' session,
Abbey Road
November 27th
German dates with
Delaney & Bonnie
December 1st–7th
British tour, Delaney &
Bonnie
December 7th
Live recording, Fairfield
Hall, Croydon
December 15th
Plastic Ono Band,
Lyceum Ballroom,
London

—

1970
February 2nd–March 3rd
Delaney & Bonnie,
North American tour

Exactly a year before the
Plastic Ono Band's second
and final appearance, Eric
had teamed up with John
and Yoko – here seen with
the Who's Keith Moon and
John Entwhistle and a
young Julian Lennon – in
the Rolling Stones'
Rock'n'Roll Circus film

PLASTIC ONO BAND

Live Peace
Toronto, Canada
September 13th 1969

Eric Clapton stayed in Los Angeles just a few days, to start organizing a solo album with the help of Delaney Bramlett. Although he had ventured tentatively into singing in the past, Eric usually took a back seat to someone else when it came to vocals, be it Keith Relf, Jack Bruce or Stevie Winwood. John Mayall had encouraged him to sing, and Stevie Winwood apparently felt Blind Faith could have been more balanced had Clapton sung his share. However, it was Delaney Bramlett who really urged him to develop his singing. The two men were very sympathetic as a team when they had off-the-cuff rehearsals and jams during both the tour and now at Delaney's home. So Clapton more or less fell in with the idea, later organized on a more formal basis, that Delaney would produce his solo debut album if Clapton accompanied the Americans on their European tour.

Backstage at the Lyceum Plastic Ono gig: Eric sits on Yoko's left in an all-star line-up that includes Bonnie and Delaney Bramlett (top right), George Harrison (centre left), Keith Moon (centre) and Billy Preston (centre right)

He flew back to London, and a couple of days after his return he received a call from John Lennon asking him to join the Plastic Ono Band on a charity gig in Toronto the next day, 13 September 1969. Clapton agreed immediately, and was met by Lennon at the airport; they rehearsed, with bass player Klaus Voorman and drummer Alan White, on board the plane to Canada, and the set list was worked out on the back of an airline menu.

The event was billed as the Toronto Rock and Roll Revival Show, and featured Little Richard, Chuck Berry, Gene Vincent and Bo Diddley as well as the Plastic Ono Band as headliners. Once backstage, John, Eric and Klaus plugged into a single

Bonnie, Delaney and Eric – Clapton's 'sitting in' tour ended in him being almost a permanent member of the band

amplifier to run through the rock'n'roll standards they had been practising at 30,000 feet; finally, around midnight, the band were introduced by singer and seminal pre-punk producer Kim Fowley.

The set kicked off with the kind of numbers John Lennon had been playing all his life — Carl Perkins' 'Blue Suede Shoes', the early Motown 'Money' and Larry Williams' 'Dizzy Miss Lizzy' — before going into the Beatles' 'Yer Blues', the debut performance of Lennon's 'Cold Turkey' and the rivetting 'Give Peace A Chance' which had already, after just a few months, become one of the anthems of the youth culture of the late 1960s. With 20,000 backing vocalists the song worked as never before.

The next two numbers, 'Don't Worry Kyoko (Mummy's Only Looking For Her Hand In The Snow)' and 'John John (Let's Hope For Peace)' were basically Yoko Ono showpieces, giving her ample opportunity to demonstrate her style of singing;

■ SET LIST ■

Blue Suede Shoes • Dizzy Miss Lizzy • Yer Blues • Cold Turkey • Give Peace A Chance • Don't Worry Kyoko • John John

The London debut of Delaney and Bonnie and Friends, on stage at the Royal Albert Hall; Eric is seen here with the Bramletts and drummer Jim Gordon

although much-derided, her improvised wailing struck a sympathetic chord with Clapton who saw it as pure self-expression, and was happy to reciprocate with some appropriate guitar contributions.

Towards the end of Yoko's set, Lennon indicated to Clapton to turn up the volume on his guitar, and leave it leaning against the amplifier, creating a howl of constant feedback. Clapton, Lennon and Voorman left the stage, leaving Yoko screaming against the barrage of noise until road manager Mal Evans switched the amps off one by one.

Eric Clapton went on to record with the Plastic Ono Band on their 'Cold Turkey' single, as well as taking part in their only other live gig, at London's Lyceum Ballroom on 15 December 1969, which included the additional musical talents of George Harrison, Delaney and Bonnie, Billy Preston, Keith Moon and others, and was recorded for release the as the live side on Lennon's 1972 *Sometime In New York City* album.

DELANEY AND BONNIE

As soon as the Blind Faith tour of North America had finished in August 1969, Clapton had done some recording with Delaney and Bonnie and Friends while working out his projected solo album with Delaney. Plans were made at that time to bring them over for a European tour which Eric agreed to take part in, and they finally arrived in the U.K. in the November, the entire band staying at Clapton's country home. For a couple of weeks they just hung out at the house, playing night and day, whenever they felt like it. It was a very laid-back way to rehearse, but as far as Eric was concerned this was a laid-back gig — just some dates with him as guest guitarist, singing some songs as well.

Billed as 'Delaney and Bonnie and Friends with

Eric Clapton', they set off for Germany where they were to appear on the country's top television pop show, 'Beatclub' and do a few dates. Unfortunately the shows were not received that well by the German audiences thanks to the promoter who advertised them solely as Eric Clapton concerts. In Cologne, the crowd was so rude that the band eventually walked off stage after performing only a few numbers.

The band's debut in England enjoyed a vastly different reception. At the first concert, at London's Albert Hall, the band was greeted with a standing ovation which did much to restore their confidence. George Harrison, who had originally introduced Clapton to Delaney Bramlett, was watching from the wings, and ended up on stage with the band. To everyone's delight, he decided to complete the further six nights of the English tour with the group, plus three nights in Copenhagen.

Both George and Eric enjoyed a degree of anonymity as bit-players in a relatively unknown band, but while as far as Clapton was concerned it was a casual arrangement, it began to be apparent that Delaney and Bonnie felt otherwise. They became increasingly dependent on his name for their own exposure; this was the burden of his celebrity status.

The tour had been fun, but it was time to plan for the future. The most obvious step was to start making plans for the long-awaited solo album. Originally it was to be called *Eric Sings*, and given the emphasis on Clapton's vocals would have been a truer guide to fans of what they were getting than the rather blander *Eric Clapton*.

Some initial tracks recorded at London's Trident Studios in the November and Olympic Studios in December were scrapped, and a fresh start made at the Village Studios in Los Angeles. Most of the songs on the album were co-written by Eric and Delaney, and although Clapton played guitar throughout, much of his lead work was buried in the mix. There were in fact at least three different mixes made, the last by Tom Dowd.

The musicians on the album included Leon Russell, some of the original Crickets who had played with one of Clapton's heroes Buddy Holly, and the Delaney and Bonnie band. There was a fresh sound that stemmed not only from the predominance of

Far left and left: *George Harrison was instrumental in Eric's eventual collaboration with Delaney and Bonnie, and six months later featured Clapton and the Delaney and Bonnie rhythm section on the sessions for his debut solo album* All Things Must Pass

vocals. Until then, Clapton's particular guitar sound had originated from a Gibson — harsh and bluesy. Now he was using a Fender Stratocaster which had a thinner and more delicate tone.

As soon as the album was finished Eric spent a month touring with Delaney and Bonnie again, this time in Canada and the United States, before heading home as the band went it's separate ways, the horn section joining the infamous 'Mad Dogs and Englishmen' tour led by Leon Russell and Joe Cocker.

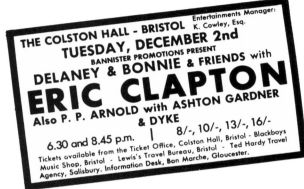

THE COLSTON HALL - BRISTOL
Entertainments Manager:
K. Cowley, Esq.
TUESDAY, DECEMBER 2nd
BANNISTER PROMOTIONS PRESENT
DELANEY & BONNIE & FRIENDS with
ERIC CLAPTON
Also P. P. ARNOLD with ASHTON GARDNER & DYKE
6.30 and 8.45 p.m. | 8/-, 10/-, 13/-, 16/-
Tickets available from the Ticket Office, Colston Hall, Bristol - Blackboys Music Shop, Bristol - Lewis's Travel Bureau, Bristol - Ted Hardy Travel Agency, Salisbury. Information Desk, Bon Marche, Gloucester.

Above: Eric with his custom-built rosewood and cedar twelve-12 string which he had made towards the end of 1969 by British guitar craftsman Tony Sematas

Right: Top rock sax player Bobby Keyes, seen here as part of the Delaney and Bonnie outfit with Eric stage left

DISCOGRAPHY

PLASTIC ONO BAND
SINGLE:
Cold Turkey (*Lennon*)/
Don't Worry Kyoko (*Ono*)
U.K. Apple 1001/U.S. Apple
1813
Abbey Road Studios,
25–28 September/3–6 October
1969
Prod. John Lennon, Yoko Ono
Released October 1969

ALBUMS:
LIVE PEACE IN TORONOTO 1969
Blue Suede Shoes (*Perkins*),
Money (*Bradford, Gordy*), **Dizzy
Miss Lizzie** (*Williams*), **Yer Blues**
(*Lennon, McCartney*), **Cold
Turkey** (*Lennon*), **Give Peace A
Chance** (*Lennon, McCartney*),
Don't Worry Kyoko (*Ono*), **John
John** (*Ono*)
U.K. Apple Core 2001/U.S.
Apple Core SW3362
Recorded live Toronto
Rock'n'Roll Revival Festival,
September 13th 1969
Prod. John Lennon, Yoko Ono
Released December 1969

SOMETIME IN NEW YORK CITY
(live side)
Cold Turkey (*Lennon*), **Don't
Worry Kyoko** (*Ono*)
U.K. Apple PCSP716/U.S. Apple
SVBB 3392
Recorded live at the Lyceum
Ballroom, London, 15 December
1969
Prod. John Lennon
Released September 1972

DELANEY AND BONNIE AND
FRIENDS
SINGLE:
Comin' Home (*B. Bramlett,
Clapton*)/
Groupie (Superstar) (*B.
Bramlett, Russell*)
Atlantic 584 308
A&M Studios, Hollywood,
September 1969
Prod. Delaney Bramlett
Released December 1969

ALBUM:
ON TOUR WITH ERIC CLAPTON
Things Get Better (*Floyd,

Cropper, Wayne), **Poor Elijah–
Tribute to Elmore Johnson
(Medley)** (*D. Bramlett, Ford/D.
Bramlett, Russell*), **Only You
Know And I Know** (*D.Mason*), **I
Don't Want To Discuss It**
(*Beatty, Cooper, Shelby*), **That's
What My Man Is For** (*B.
Griffin*), **Where There's A Will
There's A Way** (*B. Bramlett,
Whitlock*), **Coming Home** (*B.
Bramlett, Clapton*), **Little
Richard Medley – Long Tall
Sally** (*Penniman, Blackwell*),
Jenny Jenny (*Penniman*), **The
Girl Can't Help It** (*Trout*), **Tutti
Frutti** (*Penniman*)
U.K. Atlantic 2400013/U.S. Atco
SD 33-326
Recorded live at the Fairfield
Hall, Croydon, 7 December 1969
*Prod. Jimmy Miller and Delaney
Bramlett*
Released February 1970

SOLO
SINGLE:
After Midnight (*JJ Cale*)/
Easy Now (*Clapton*)
U.K. Polydor 2001 096
Village Recorders, LA January
1970
Prod. Delaney Bramlett
Released August 1970

ALBUM:
ERIC CLAPTON
Slunky (*Bramlett, Clapton*) **Bad
Boy** (*Bramlett, Clapton*), **Told
You For The Last Time**
(*Bramlett, Cropper*), **After
Midnight** (*Cale*), **Easy Now**
(*Clapton*), **Blues Power** (*Clapton,
Russell*), **Bottle of Red Wine**
(*Bramlett, Clapton*), **Lovin' You
Lovin'Me** (*Bramlett, Clapton*),
**Lonseome And A Long Way
From Home** (*Bramlett, Russell*),
Don't Know Why (*Bramlett,
Clapton*), **Let It Rain** (*Bramlett,
Clapton*)
U.K. Polydor 238021/U.S. Atco
SD 33329
Village Recorders, LA January
1970
Prod. Delaney Bramlett
Released August 1970

Atlantic
has nothing to say...
except
DELANEY & BONNIE
& FRIENDS
ON TOUR
WITH ERIC CLAPTON
or maybe
LED ZEPPELIN?..... CROSBY, STILLS, NASH & YOUNG?..... LORD SUTCH?
'Led Zeppelin 2'   'Déjà Vu'   '& Heavy Friends'

TOURS

1969
November
27th Frankfurt **28th** Hamburg
29th Cologne
December
1st Royal Albert Hall, London
2nd Colston Hall, Bristol **3rd**
Town Hall, Birmingham **4th** City
Hall, Sheffield **5th** City Hall,
Newcastle **6th** Empire Theatre,
Liverpool **7th** Fairfield Hall,
Croydon

1970
February
2nd Massey Hall, Tornoto **5th**
'Dick Cavett Show', ABC TV,
New York **6&7th** Fillmore East,
New York **8&9th** Tea Party
Boston **11th** Electric Factory,
Philadelphia **12th** Symphony
Hall, Minneapolis **14th**
Auditorium Theatre, Chicago
15th Memorial Hall, Kansas
19–22nd Fillmore West, San
Francisco
March
3rd Civic Auditorium, Santa
Monica

DEREK AND THE DOMINOS

*T*he period with Eric as Derek was not an entirely happy one. Although he was enjoying a new freedom in many ways, his life was being increasingly ruled by a more insidious constraint, hard drugs.

Furthermore, the period was overshadowed not only by heroin, but death. His grandfather died just weeks after the demise of Eric's friend, fellow guitar genius Jimi Hendrix, and Duane Allman, who collaborated on the Dominos' album and briefly joined the band, was killed on a motorcycle not long after.

Session activity was highlighted by the tracks on George Harrison's solo debut, and the now-legendary 'London Sessions' with one of Eric's original heroes, Howlin' Wolf Burnett.

Although the band itself broke up in something of a shambles, most of the members having a drug habit, it had in its early stages produced one of the vinyl high spots of Clapton's career — the track 'Layla', one of the few enduring love songs to come out of the modern rock scene.

DIARY

—

1970
January
Records solo album,
Village Studios, LA
May–July
George Harrison's *All
Things Must Pass* LP
June
Domino's debut single
produced by Phil
Spector
June 14th–August 2nd
U.K. debut tour
July
Howlin' Wolf's 'London
Sessions' LP
**August 22nd–
September 2nd**
Recording album,
including 'Layla', Miami
Florida
**September 11th–
October 11th**
Second U.K. tour
**October 15th–
December 6th**
U.S. tour

—

1971
April
Dominos break up
during recording
sessions

*Eric and the Dominos,
with Bobby Whitlock
looking over the piano*

ALL THINGS MUST PASS

Domino debut
Lyceum Ballroom, London
June 14th 1970

March and April 1970 was mostly spent in London with Bill Halverson mixing and editing the tapes of his solo album. One day early in April Clapton got a call from Carl Radle, who had been bass player with the Delaney and Bonnie band. Radle told him that he, along with Bobby Whitlock and Jim Gordon — all of whom had been in the Joe Cocker 'Mad Dogs' circus — were interested in forming a band. Clapton invited them to fly over and stay at his house, to see if something might work out, and while they were rehearsing in this way George Harrison asked them to contribute to his solo album *All Things Must Pass*, which commenced recording at London's Abbey Road Studios in May 1970.

The Harrison album session lasted until the end of July, under the meticulous supervision of Phil Spector. Clapton played on about a third of the tracks, though the others in his new line-up played throughout. Other session work that kept Clapton busy at this time included albums by Steven Stills, Doris Troy, Ashton Gardner and Dyke and the memorable *London Sessions* with blues giant Howlin' Wolf that also included, among others, Steve Winwood, Bill Wyman and Ringo Starr.

On 14 June the new band, glorying in the name Derek and the Dominos, made its first public appearance at London's Lyceum Ballroom. This Lyceum show also featured Dave Mason on guitar although he was not to be a permanent fixture as he too would shortly be embarking on a solo career.

Towards the end of the Harrison sessions they recorded their first single 'Tell The Truth' and 'Roll It Over' with Phil Spector at the controls and George helping out on guitar. Although the single was released, the band had it withdrawn from the shops after a few days beacuse they were not satisfied with the end result; it was replaced by 'After Midnight' from Clapton's solo album that had just been released.

LAYLA

A low-key British tour of the club and ballroom circuit ran through the first three weeks of August, before the band took off for the Criteria Studios in Miami to record an album that would be called *Layla and Other Assorted Love Songs*. The first few days were spent just jamming and thinking of material to include; 'Derek' had already been working for about a year on the title track, which was obliquely dedicated to George Harrison's wife Patti with whom he had fallen hopelessly in love. The other numbers, some originals and some blues standards, developed in the studio.

The sessions were produced by Atlantic's Tom Dowd who had worked with Cream, and a highlight of the project for Clapton was the involvement of Duane Allman on guitar. They admired each other's work; Allman had rated Clapton since his work with the Bluesbreakers, and likewise the Englishman had been longing to meet the man who had made such eloquent contributions to records by the likes of Aretha Franklin and Wilson Pickett.

Dowd had introduced the guitarists at an Allman Brothers Band show in Miami, and after visiting the studio the next day Duane was asked if he would like to take part in the sessions. Duane originated from Macon, Georgia, and with his brother Gregg, taught himself to play guitar by listening to the work of blues masters such as Muddy Waters, Robert Johnson and Blind Lemon Jefferson. Their first band was called

The Lyceum debut night, with (left to right) Whitlock away from the keyboards, Clapton and Dave Mason, as an accoustic trio

Radle and Clapton (**far left**) during the Dominos' only American tour late in 1970, Eric deciding (**left**) to 'wrap up' in jumper and scarf some nights!

the Allman Joys, later changed to Hour Glass and then the Allman Brothers Band.

So close a musical liaison did he and Clapton forge during the 'Layla' sessions, that he was considering going on the road with the Dominos. In the end he decided to stay with his brother, though he did join Eric's band for a few gigs a month or so later. Tragically, he was to die the following year in a motorcycle accident.

After the sessions Eric and the band returned for the next leg of their British tour. Clapton had recently purchased a rare left-handed Fender Stratocaster for his friend Jimi Hendrix who always played a right-handed one upside down. They were to meet after a show by Sly and the Family Stone at the Lyceum, but Hendrix never showed up. It was not until later that

Clapton learned that Jimi had died that night. By coincidence, Clapton had recorded Jimi's 'Little Wing' nine days before his death during the Dominos' sessions in Miami, so he included it as an onstage tribute to Hendrix for the duration of the tour, which ended at the Lyceum on 11 October.

ROLL IT OVER

*T*wo days later they flew to the States for their only American tour. Four shows were recorded at the Fillmore East, New York, though nothing was released of the material until 1973. Then early in November they appeared on the Johnny Cash television show from Nashville performing a version of 'It's Too Late' before being joined by both the host and Carl Perkins for a version of the latter's 'Matchbox'. Short of any bootlegs that may exist, the Cash show tape is the only known video or film footage of the Dominos in action.

■ SET LIST ■

Why Does Love Got To Be So Sad? • Tell The Truth • Blues Power • Have You Ever Loved A Woman? • Keep On Growing • Nobody Loves you When Your Down And Out • Bottle Of Red Wine • Little Wing • Roll It Over • Bell Bottom Blues • Let It Rain

The Dominos – Bobby Whitlock, Eric, Jim Gordon and Carl Radle – during the American concert trek

Eric found it harder and harder to really relax during the gruelling U.S. schedules

Halfway through the tour another blow to Eric was the death of his grandfather. Robert Stigwood had called Eric to tell him of his grandfather's critical illness, and he flew home immediately to be with his family although he had to return to the U.S.A. after a few days to resume the tour.

There was a bizarre incident at the Civic Auditorium, Santa Monica, when Delaney Bramlett got up to jam with the band. As if trying to prove his authority over the musicians he may have felt Eric had 'stolen' (though in fact they had left Delaney to join Joe Cocker's tour), he swamped the whole proceedings by a sheer excess of volume. Needless to say, he was not invited to appear with them again.

This was not a good period for the Dominos in many ways. From around the time of the George Harrison sessions, Eric had been using hard drugs with increasing frequency, and the same was true of the rest of the band. By the end of the American trek they were all fairly strung out most of the time, and this was evident when they got together back in England in April 1971 to record their second album.

A strained lack of direction showed itself in the music, which consisted of long jams, half-finished instrumentals and some fairly predictable blues standards. The band broke up halfway through the sessions in May after an argument between Eric and Jim Gordon, though a couple of tracks turned up later in re-recorded form: 'High' on the *One In Every Crowd* album, and 'Mean Old Frisco' on *Slowhand*.

■ SET LIST ■

Got To Get Better • Roll It Over • Blues Power • Why Does Love Got To Be So Sad • Tell The Truth • Stormy Monday • Little Wing • Have You Ever Loved A Woman • Little Queenie • Let It Rain • Everyday I Have The Blues • Bottle Of Red Wine • Sweet Little Rock'n'Roller • Nobody Loves You When You're Down and Out • Crossroads • Key To The Highway

DISCOGRAPHY

SINGLES:
Tell The Truth (*Clapton, Whitlock*)/
Roll It Over (*Clapton, Bramlett*)
U.K. Polydor 2058057/U.S. Atco
456780
Trident Studios, London,
June 1970
Prod. Phil Spector
Released September 1970

Layla (*Clapton, Gordon*)/
Bell Bottom Blues (*Clapton*)
U.K. Polydor 2058130/U.S. Atco
6809
Criteria Studios, Miami,
27 August–2 October 1970
*Prod. Tom Dowd and the
Dominos*
Released November 1970

ALBUMS:
**LAYLA AND OTHER ASSORTED
LOVE SONGS**
I Looked Away (*Clapton,
Whitlock*), **Bell Bottom Blues**
(*Clapton*), **Keep On Growing**
(*Clapton, Whitlock*), **Nobody
Loves You When You're Down
And Out** (*Cox*), **I Am Yours**
(*Clapton, Nizami*), **Anyday**
(*Clapton, Whitlock*), **Key To The
Highway** (*Seeger, Broonzy*), **Tell
The Truth** (*Clapton, Whitlock*),
**Why Does Love Got To Be So
Sad?** (*Clapton, Whitlock*), **Have
You Ever Loved A Woman?**
(*Myles*), **Little Wing** (*Hendrix*),
It's Too Late (*Willis*), **Layla**
(*Clapton, Gordon*), **Thorn Tree
In The Garden** (*Whitlock*)
U.K. Polydor 2625005/U.S. Atco
SD 2704
Criteria Studios, Miami,
27 August–2 October 1970
*Prod. Tom Dowd and the
Dominos*
Released December 1970

IN CONCERT
**Why Does Love Got To Be So
Sad?** (*Clapton, Whitlock*), **Got To
Get Better In A Little While**
(*Clapton*), **Let It Rain** (*Clapton,
Bramlett*), **Presence Of The Lord**
(*Clapton*), **Tell The Truth**

(*Clapton, Whitlock*), **Bottle Of
Red Wine** (*Clapton, Bramlett*),
Roll It Over (*Clapton, Bramlett*),
Blues Power (*Clapton, Russell*),
**Have You Ever Loved A
Woman?** (*Myles*)
U.K. RSO 2659020/U.S. RSO
502-8800
Recorded live at the Fillmore
East, New York
23–24 October 1970
Prod. Andy Knight
Released March 1973

TOURS

1970
June
14th Lyceum Ballroom, London
August
1st Roundhouse, London **2nd** The
Place, Hanley **7th** Mecca
Ballroom, Newcastle **8th**
California Ballroom, Dunstable
9th Mothers, Birmingham **11th**
Marquee, London **12th**
Speakeasy, London **14th** Winter
Gardens, Malvern **15th** Tofts,
Folkestone **16th** Black Prince,
Bexley **18th** Pavilion,
Bournemouth **21st** Town Hall,
Torquay **22nd** Van Dyke Club,
Plymouth
September
11th Marquee, London **20th**
Fairfield Hall, Croydon **21st** De
Montfort Hall, Leicester **23rd**
Dome, Brighton **24th**
Philharmonic Hall, Liverpool
25th Greens Playhouse, Glasgow
27 Colston Hall, Bristol **28th** Free
Trade Hall, Manchester
October
5th Town Hall, Birmingham **7th**
Winter Gardens, Bournemouth
8th Leeds University **9th**
Penthouse, Scarborough **11th**
Lyceum Ballroom, London
15th Rider College, Trenton,
New Jersey **16–17th** Electric
Factory, Philadelphia **21st**

George Washington University,
Washington DC **23–24th**
Fillmore East, New York **29th**
Kleinhaus Music Hall, Buffalo
30th Albany University, Albany
31st Victoria Beach Dome,
Virginia Beach
November
1st Civic Auditorium,
Jacksonville **5th** Johnny Cash
T.V. show, Nashville **6th**
McFarlin Auditorium, Dallas **7th**
Community Center Theater, San
Antonio **13th** Nevada University,
Reno **14th** Fairgrounds Coliseum,
Salt Lake City **17th** Memorial
Auditorium, Sacramento **18–19th**
Community Theater, Berkeley
20th Civic Auditorium, Santa
Monica **21st** Civic Auditorium,
Pasadena **22nd** Community
Concourse, San Diego **25th**
Auditorium Theater, Chicago
26th Music Hall, Cincinnati **27th**
Keil Opera House, St Louis **28th**
Music Hall, Cleveland **29th**
Painters Mill Music Fair, Owings
Mills, Maryland
December
1st Curtis Hixon Hall, Tampa **2nd**
War Memorial Auditorium,
Syracuse **3rd** East Town
Theater, Detroit **4–5th** Capitol
Theater, Porchester, New York
6th Suffolk Community College,
Seldon, New York

OFF THE
ROAD

*F*ourteen years before Live Aid, The Concert For Bangla Desh was the first large-scale 'charity' concert involving rock music, conceived and organised by Eric's friend George Harrison.

During the time Eric was living the life of a recluse, Harrison was one of his few regular visitors. He was worried about Clapton's state of health, mentally and physically, and was eager to involve his friend in whatever projects might be in the pipeline, only if to 'get him out' into the real world.

Despite 'Bangla Desh' being a huge success — the live concert, film and subsequent boxed record set — and his brief reappearance in the international spotlight, again Eric did what amounted to a disappearing act; it was a year later when he was once more dragged out of hibernation by musical friends and colleagues concerned about his well-being.

*George Harrison, with
Clapton to his left, at the
Concert For Bangla Desh
which he conceived and
put together*

IT DON'T COME EASY

Concert for Bangla Desh
Madison Square Garden, NYC
August 1st 1971

August 1971; as far as the general public was concerned, Eric Clapton had done nothing since the end of 1970, although he had been playing sessions, recording the last Dominos tracks and writing a few songs or parts of songs.

Nevertheless, it would be true to say that this was a period of relative inactivity, brought about in the main by Clapton's increasing dependence on heroin. He was quite content to stay ensconced in his mansion, doodling on the guitar, visited regularly by George Harrison and a close circle of friends he allowed in — many callers were simply ignored. He relied on his girlfriend Alice Ormsby-Gore, herself also an addict, to keep things more or less together. In fact, this situation persisted until early in 1973, apart from a spectacular event organized by George Harrison, the Concert For Bangla Desh.

In aid of the starving people of that country, in many ways a precursor of the Live Aid concerts of the 1980s, it was held at New York's Madison Square Garden on 1 August 1971. Indian sitar virtuoso and Harrison's musical guru Ravi Shankar opened the

concert, followed onstage by an all-star line up of George Harrison, Eric Clapton, Jesse Davis and Don Preston on guitars, Ringo Starr and Jim Keltner on drums, Leon Russell on piano, bass player Klaus Voorman, Billy Preston on organ, and backing vocals from Apple protégés Badfinger.

Each artist did one of his own songs, backed by the others. Clapton's main contribution was his solo on 'When My Guitar Gently Weeps', plus of course significant backing throughout.

The most celebrated guest appearance on the show was that of Bob Dylan, backed by Russell, Starr and Harrison. There were two concerts, afternoon and evening, and both were filmed and recorded for later release. Clapton was greeted with a huge ovation when he was introduced, but the audience was unaware of the physical torment he was going through.

His heroin supply was not as easy to come by as at home, and he was suffering from severe withdrawal symptoms that prevented him from even attending any of the rehearsals. Eventually he was given a morphine-based substitute which enabled him to make the actual concerts, after which he returned home not to appear in public again for some months.

Apart from a one-off gig with Leon Russell, when he appeared unannounced at London's Rainbow Theatre on 4 December 1971, Clapton made no other public appearances for more than a year. He did accept an invitation to take part in a Stevie Wonder recording at Air Studios in London in October 1972, but no material from the sessions subsequently appeared in any form. But 1972 and 1973 were wilderness years for this great guitarist and the question was being asked: Could he ever recapture his earlier majestic skills? Could he come through his torment?

The concert was the culmination of months of planning, hustling and hoping for former-Beatle Harrison, who also saw it as an opportunity for his friend Eric Clapton to reappear on the public stage

■ SET LIST ■
Eric played on the following numbers:

Wah Wah • My Sweet Lord • Awaiting On You All • That's The Way God Planned It • It Don't Come Easy • Beware of Darkness • While My Guitar Gently Weeps • Jumpin' Jack Flash • Young Blood • Something • Bangla Desh

THE COMEBACK

A regular source of support to Eric and Alice at this time, as well as George Harrison, was the Who's Pete Townshend. Just before the Stevie Wonder session they had attended a Who concert in Paris at Pete's invitation and visited Keith Richards at his home in Villefranche in the South of France. On their return Alice's father, Lord Harlech — who was concerned in a positive way for them both to cure their drug problem — asked Pete Townshend to organize a band to back Clapton for a concert planned for January 1973. The event was part of 'Fanfare For Europe', celebrating Britain's entry into the Common Market. His idea was to bring Clapton back into the public arena and, he hoped,

give him the incentive to kick the drug habit. Clapton finally agreed to take part after much persuading by Alice and Pete.

Getting other musicians to participate raised little difficulty. Eventually, Townshend settled on Stevie Winwood, Ronnie Wood, Rick Grech, drummers Jim Capaldi and Jimmy Karstein and percussionist Rebop. Rehearsals took place at Ronnie Wood's home, The Wick, at the top of Richmond Hill, near London, before heading out for a final run through at Guildford's Civic Hall.

The two concerts took place at the Rainbow Theatre in London on 13 January at 6.30 and 8.30pm. Ticket agencies were inundated with customers, many of whom had queued all night before the day they went on sale, and the two shows were sold out within hours. The first concert was delayed due to Clapton's late arrival. Alice had been making last-minute adjustments to his suit which needed 'letting

A Rainbow coalition: Stevie Winwood, Ron Wood, Pete Townshend and Clapton in full flight during Eric's 'comeback' concert

out' after his gaining weight over the previous two years, and everyone was aware that Eric's own state of health was hardly a guarantee of reliability. For Robert Stigwood and Pete Townshend in particular, it was nail-biting time until he arrived at the stage door.

For Clapton, the tension was undoubtedly heightened by the presence of friends in the audience including Jimmy Page, George Harrison, Ringo Starr, Elton John and Joe Cocker, all there to witness and encourage his return to the concert stage. Whatever nervousness he may have experienced, and which he admitted to afterwards, was not apparent in his performance. His playing was at times restrained but always authoritative, and the whole band was certainly on form.

Both concerts were recorded by the Ronnie Lane mobile studio and an album released in the September of that year. Some of the best music of the evening did not make it on to the album, but at the time of writing there were plans for a C.D. release of the previously unavailable material.

Pete Townshend, like George Harrison, stuck by Eric through his difficult patches and organized the Rainbow event from concept to concert. The two lead players (right) with very different styles, trade licks, while (far right) Stevie Winwood, Ron Wood, Rick Grech, Eric and Pete Townshend encore on 'Crossroads'

■ *SET LIST* ■

Layla • Badge • Blues Power • Nobody Loves You When You're Down And Out • Roll It Over • Why Does Your Love Got To Be So Sad • Little Wing • Bottle Of Red Wine • After Midnight • Bell Bottom Blues (*1st show only*) • Presence Of The Lord • Tell The Truth • Pearly Queen • Key To The Highway (*2nd show only*) • Let It Rain • Crossroads

■ D I S C O G R A P H Y ■

ALBUM
THE RAINBOW CONCERT
Badge *(Clapton, Harrison)*, **Roll
It Over** *(Clapton, Whitlock)*,
Presence Of The Lord *(Clapton)*,
Pearly Queen *(Winwood,
Capaldi)*, **After Midnight** *(Cale)*,
Little Wing *(Hendrix)*
U.K. RSO 2394116/U.S.
RSO 50877
Recorded live at the
Rainbow Theatre, London,
13 January 1973
Prod. Bob Pridden
Released September 1973

GOING SOLO

*T*he solo years of the Seventies saw a Clapton renaissance. Right from the *'461 Ocean Boulevard* album of 1974, it was clear his playing — and singing — had taken on a new lease of life. He now had a backing band of world class quality, although on 'Boulevard' they were allowed plenty of up-front blowing, even to the neglect of Eric's solos some fans felt.

The touring schedules, especially in North America, were as heavy as in the heyday of Cream, punctuated by recording stints that produced another four highly acclaimed studio albums before the end of the decade.

Things were changing as the Eighties approached, however. The punk backlash of '76 regarded Eric's generation of rock stars as dinosaurs, relics of the late Sixties still being trundled round American auditoria in convoys of trucks manned by beer-bellied roadies.

Once again, change was on the agenda of Clapton's kaleideoscopic career.

DIARY

1971
February
Commences heroin cure with
Dr Meg Patterson
April 10th 'Comeback' album
and tour announced
April–May
Recording, Criteria Studios, Miami
June 28th–August 4th
U.S. tour
October 31st–November 6th
Japanese tour
November 26th–December 5th
European tour
December
Shooting Ken Russell's film of
Tommy

1975
April 7th–28th
Australasian tour
June 14th–August 30th
U.S. tour
July 28th
Session for Bob Dylan's 'Desire'
LP
September 12th
'Circasia' charity film
October 22nd–November 2nd
2nd tour of Japan

1976
July 27th–August 17th
U.K. tour
November 5th–22nd
U.S. tour
November 26th
The Last Waltz concert and film.

1977
April 8th–29th
U.K. tour
June 4th–21st
European tour
September 26th–October 9th
Japanese tour

1978
Feburary 1st–April 9th
U.S. tour
June 23rd
Feÿenourd Stadium,
Rotterdam with Bob Dylan
July 1st
Nuremburg Festival with Bob Dylan
July 15th
Blackbushe Festival, U.K.,
with Bob Dylan
November 5th
Tour of Europe and U.K.

1979
March 8th–17th
Irish tour
March 27th
Marries Patti Boyd, Tucson
Arizona
March 28th–June 24th
U.S. tour
July
Rehearses all-British band
October 6th–December 6th
Tour of Eastern Europe, Israel
and Far East

OCEAN BOULEVARD

Comeback tour commences
Yale Bowl, Newhaven, Conn.
June 28th 1974

Although the Rainbow concerts were successful on a musical level, unfortunately they did not succeed in getting Eric Clapton off heroin. He was still clinging to his addiction and remained in the abyss until February 1974 when both he and Alice finally agreed to go for a cure after pressure from Lord Harlech. The treatment took the form of electro-acupuncture to deaden the pain of withdrawal symptoms and had been brought to England from Hong Kong by Dr. Meg Patterson. It was a fairly new method and had not been fully developed, but Clapton agreed that the doctor should move into his home for a week of treatment.

That he now wanted to be cured was obviously the most important factor. It was decided that the best way to help he and Alice was to split them up, Alice going to a special clinic and Eric to the Harley Street home of Meg Patterson and her husband, George. It was a rough time, but after a month he was ready to leave and continue his recuperation. Part of this process involved going to Alice's brothers' farm in Wales to work for a month as a farm hand during the day, writing material in the evenings and going to the pub to get drunk.

Preceeding page: Eric on his comeback tour of 1974

Below: with Pete Townshend and Elton John on the night of the tour announcement at the China Garden restaurant

The split from Alice on medical grounds made them both realize that a final emotional separation was inevitable, and Clapton's thoughts once again turned to Patti Harrison. But Patti remained with George, not yet ready to leave him, even though their relationship was slowly breaking up. Eric knew he could not allow himself to stay at home and vegetate and wanted to prove his new confidence in himself by recording a new album, getting a band together and touring the world. Before he could do this, however, he had made his mind up to once again pursue Patti, even going as far as telling George of his feelings. She eventually joined Eric on his long American tour, giving the press much to gossip about.

On 10 April 1974, Robert Stigwood organized a comeback party for Clapton at The China Garden Restaurant in Soho, London, announcing that he would be flying out to Criteria Studios in Miami to record his new album, followed by a U.S. tour and some English dates toward the end of the year. To help him celebrate were friends including Pete Townshend, Elton John and Ronnie Wood. Once in Miami, Clapton met his old Domino bass player Carl Radle who had stayed in touch since their split in 1971. Radle recommended drummer Jamie Oldaker and organist Dick Sims, and producer Tom Dowd brought in guitarist George Terry, keyboard player Alby Galuten and Yvonne Elliman to complete the line up for Clapton's band.

Eric had no firm plans for his album except that it should be different to all previous ones. They recorded quite a few instrumental blues jams to get into the groove. However, much of the tracks with guitar solos were left off the final album in order to make a decisive break from the guitar hero label that Clapton had worn all these years. Quite a few songs came about by accident. George Terry had introduced Clapton to the *Burnin'* album by Bob Marley and the Wailers and it was decided to do a cover of his song 'I Shot The Sheriff' taken from that album. Released as a single, this became Eric's first No. 1 in America.

Once the sessions were completed, Robert Stigwood arranged a huge American tour to promote his new album, which had been given the title *461 Ocean Boulevard* after the residence they were staying at on Miami's Golden Beach. Roger Forrester, now Clapton's manager, was at that time an associate of Stigwood's and had tried to persuade him not to send

The opening night at New Haven, Conneticut (**far left**) marked the eccentricity of Eric's appearance on much of the tour, rivalled only by that of compere 'Legs' Larry (**left**)

Clapton out on such a large tour so soon after his return from ill health. He was overruled and the multi-million dollar tour went ahead as planned. The opening date was at the Yale Bowl in New Haven, Connecticut on 28 June.

Alcohol had now replaced heroin in his life and the pressures of playing the large arenas and stadiums, staying in endless hotels and travelling long distances did nothing to help matters. Eric's behaviour during the early part of the tour was eccentric to say the least. He would arrive on stage wearing a see-through plastic mac with a hotel 'Do Not Disturb' tag attached to it. On another occasion, he had half a dozen daffodils hanging out of his jacket pocket.

His eccentricity was no doubt fuelled by ex-Bonzo Dog Doo Dah Band member 'Legs' Larry Smith who was brought along to introduce Clapton and his band. The lights went down and suddenly the Who's 'Pinball Wizard' came throught the PA at full volume, quickly followed by 'Legs' bounding on stage, normally dressed in an outrageous polka dot outfit, or similar, and clutching a little orange ukelele doing a Pete Townshend impersonation, after which he would introduce Eric Clapton.

The crowds loved it, but their enthusiasm some-times got out of hand and they would throw fire-crackers, or worse, bottles at the stage. On one occasion in Providence, a beer bottle hit Yvonne Elliman on the hand. Rather than getting angry, Clapton politely asked the people responsible to calm

■ SET LIST ■

U.S.A Tour part 1 28th June–4th August 1974
Set list taken from the following and would differ nightly:

Smile • Easy Now • Let It Grow • Can't Find My Home • Don't Have To Hurt Nobody • I Shot The Sheriff • Willie And The Hand Jive • Get Ready • Presence Of The Lord • Drifting Blues • Steady Rollin' Man • Mainline Florida • Have You Ever Loved A Woman • Blues Power • I Can't Hold Out • Let It Rain • Tell The Truth • Mean Old World • Bright Lights Big City • Matchbox • Key To The Highway • Badge • Little Wing • Layla • Crossroads • Little Queenie

down and proceeded to do a blues number, 'Don't Have To Hurt Nobody' which did more good than had he stormed off stage. (Normally, Eric would open the set with Charlie Chaplin's 'Smile', one of his favourite songs, from Chaplin's film *Modern Times*.)

The tour was gruelling, often consisting of two shows in one day to meet the spectacular ticket demand. The early shows, particularly the warm-ups in Stockholm and Copenhagen, showed that the band needed to tighten up as a musical entity, as did the first few shows in America. This was to do both with Eric's rustiness and his excessive consumption of alcohol as was widely reported. He had not toured since 1970 with the Dominos, or indeed had a permanent band. Although he was drinking heavily, he was able to play.

The sets differed every night and as the band got to know themselves better musically, the length and variety of numbers changed regularly. Just listen to the live version of 'Have You Ever Loved A Woman' on *EC Was Here* and hear the amazing interplay between Clapton and George Terry.

Quite a few guests jammed with them such as Freddie King in Buffalo, where Clapton also sat in with the supporting act, the Band. King also put in a memorable peformance of 'Have You Ever Loved A Woman' at the Roosevelt Stadium in New Jersey. Other guests included Todd Rundgren on 'Little Queenie' at Madison Square Garden in New York, John Mayall at the Long Beach Arena in California

As the tour progressed, Clapton's sartorial flamboyance subsided. By the time they played Nassau, Long Island, at the end of June (**above right**), he was wearing a suit!

(where two shows were taped by RSO), Pete Townshend at the Omni in Atlanta when he and Clapton performed a version of 'Baby Don't You Do It' with Keith Moon joining the proceedings on 'Little Queenie'. The Who men also joined in at the Coliseum, in Greensboro and at the West Palm Beach International Raceway. The encore most nights would be 'Little Queenie' which featured a memorable tap dance routine by master of ceremonies 'Legs' Larry Smith, with every step faithfully replayed through the PA system!

As soon as the American tour ended on 4 August, Clapton and his band went back to Criteria Studios in Miami to play on a session with Freddie King, who had now been signed to Robert Stigwood's label RSO. King had been a longtime influence on Clapton, being one of the first electric blues guitarists he had heard. In fact it was a photo on one of his album

Left: *The American tour was preceded by a short visit to Scandinavia, including a gig in the fairground venue of Gronaland in Stockholm*

The Copenhagen gig: (**right**) rehearsing, (**far right**) with Yvonne Elliman sharing the vocals (**below**) and Eric encouraging drummer Jamie Oldaker (**opposite top**)

Opposite bottom left: The Madison Square Garden dates were a highspot of the American trek.
Opposite bottom right: At Madison Square Garden Eric introduces guitarist George Terry

covers holding a Gibson Les Paul, that led the Englishman to buy one like it.

At the end of August, two and a half weeks of studio time were booked at Dymanic Sounds in Kingston, Jamaica for sessions for the next Clapton album. Fourteen tracks were completed including two with ex-Wailer Peter Tosh on vocals and guitar. A further track 'Opposites' was recorded later at Criteria. These sessions featured some of Eric's best work covering various styles such as gospel, blues and reggae. In fact, he wrote a sequel to Bob Marley's 'I Shot The Sheriff' called 'Don't Blame Me (I Didn't Shoot No Deputy)'.

461 Ocean Boulevard had been released in August to almost universal critical acclaim and sold in vast quantities worldwide. To promote it, further American dates were arranged for September and October, followed by Japan, Europe and finally two memorable shows (recorded live for possible late release) at the Hammersmith Odeon in London on 4 and 5 December 1974. There Ronnie Wood joined Eric for the two encores on the second gig. Another vocalist, Marcy Levy, had joined the band for the

*The comeback 1974 was certainly some comeback. The American tours had been followed by the Far East and Europe, climaxing in London. American dates included Madison Square Garden where Eric was joined by Todd Rundgren (**opposite left**) while the European dates took him once again to Paris (**below**)*

Jamaican sessions and stayed on full time. The tour gave them the opportunity to perform numbers just recorded such as 'The Sky Is Crying', 'Better Make It Through Today', and 'Little Rachel'.

Around this time the newly-energetic star also managed to fit in rehearsals for his first film performance, as the preacher in Ken Russell's version of the Who's *Tommy*. So 1974 ended on a high creative note, and 'Slowhand' was back.

E.C. WAS HERE

Eric started 1975 by playing on a session for Arthur Louis at Essex Sound Studios including a reggae version of 'Knockin' On Heaven's Door'. His new album, *There's One In Every Crowd* was released in April, but was commercially disappointing, perhaps because the public was not yet ready for its diversity of style. As he was now in a high tax bracket, Clapton was advised to

Above: *The London dates that ended 1974 saw the addition of vocalist Marcy Levy, seen on the right*

Right: *Eric was simply playing better than ever before, with* Ocean Boulevard *his recent success*

spend a year out of the Britain, basing himself and Patti in Nassau in the Bahamas, although most of the tax year was spent touring.

Eric Clapton toured Hawaii, New Zealand and Australia, before heading back to the Bahamas, then another huge American tour was lined up starting in June and lasting through to the end of August with a short break in the middle. The only song performed from his new album was 'Better Make It Through Today' with the remainder of the set being a mixture of old favourites from the *Layla* album such as 'Keep On Growing', 'Bell Bottom Blues', 'Tell The Truth', 'Key To The Highway' and of course 'Layla' itself which normally opened the show. Other numbers would include 'Stormy Monday', 'Knockin' On Heaven's Door', 'Badge', 'Little Wing', 'Further On Up The Road', and a new song called 'Carnival To Rio', the encore was 'Eyesight To The Blind' which would feature Carlos Santana in some inspired guitar interplay with Clapton. As on the 1974 tour, the set would differ every night which kept all the players on their toes.

In New York Eric met the Rolling Stones who were also touring the States, promoting their *Black*

Clapton's patchwork shirt was another fashion talking point for the Hammersmith punters who'd grown bored with agreeing how great the music was!

and Blue album. They jammed together at Madison Square Garden on 22 June on 'Sympathy For The Devil'. The Stones returned the compliment by attending one of Clapton's recording sessions at Jimi Hendrix's Electric Lady Studios in Greenwich Village. They ran through several takes of 'Carnival To Rio', featuring Mick Jagger on vocals, Billy Preston on

■ SET LIST ■

Set for U.S.A and Japan 1975 tour was taken from the following and would differ nightly:

Layla • Bell Bottom Blues • Key To The Highway • Mainline Florida • Keep On Growing • Can't Find My Way Home • Carnival • Stormy Monday • Little Wing • Tell The Truth • Why Does Love Got To Be So Sad • Teach Me To Be Your Woman • Badge • Let It Rain • Blues Power • Knockin' On Heaven's Door • Further On Up The Road • Eyesight To The Blind

Hammersmith Odeon – a triumphant end to 1974!

The film star! Eric as the Preacher in the Ken Russell movie version of the Who's Tommy

On tour with Roger Forrester (right), now his manager

Above: *June 1975, Madison Square Garden, New York; Clapton jams with the Rolling Stones*

Left: *Keith shares a joke while Ronnie Wood looks on*

Hangin' loose backstage –
Eric and organ virtuoso
Richard 'Dick' Sims cover for
each other as the paparazzi
close in

clavinet, Dick Sims on organ, Marcy Levy and Yvonne Elliman on vocals, Jamie Oldaker and Charlie Watts on drums, Bill Wyman and Carl Radle on bass, Ollie Brown on congos, Keith Richards, Ronnie Wood and George Terry on guitars and finally Eric Clapton himself on lead vocals and guitar. Some line-up. Needless to say, they were all fairly drunk, but the result does sound great and lasts for around eight minutes, with each guitarist taking his turn to solo. It was never released because of the contractual difficulties involved and was re-recorded in early 1976 for the *No Reason To Cry* sessions and its title shortened to 'Carnival'.

The other number that Clapton recorded at the New York sessions was 'Someone Like You' and was eventually released as the B side to 'Knockin' On Heaven's Door' single. Incidentally Bob Dylan had heard the Clapton version of his song, and obviously approved, because on 28 July he asked the Englishman to play slide on 'Romance In Durango' at Columbia Studios, New York, which was to be a track for Bob's up-coming album *Desire*.

Eric Clapton returned to England for a short visit in early September, taking in a show by his friend Santana at Hammersmith Odeon in London. He then went to County Kildare in Ireland where he took part in a film featuring various famous stars dressed as clowns, including Richard Harris, Shirley Maclaine, Judy Geeson and Burgess Meredith. The film was called *Circasia* and was in aid of the Central Remedial Clinic and the Variety Club of Ireland.

EC Was Here, a live album recorded at Long Beach Arena, Hammersmith Odeon and Nassau Coliseum was released in September, giving guitar fans what they wanted, an electric blues album. Clapton was not keen on the idea but eventually agreed to its release after hearing the version of 'Have You Ever Loved A Woman' that Tom Dowd wanted to use for the project. It is worth noting that the compact disc release of this album includes the full version of 'Driftin' Blues' which faded out after a few minutes on the original release.

SHANGRI-LA

In late October, he toured Japan for the second time, after which it was time for a break from what had been a punishing schedule. Ronnie Wood had flown out to stay with Eric at his rented house in the Bahamas to try and work on some songs for the new Clapton album which was shortly to be recorded. Not much was done, maybe two half-finished numbers, the main reason being Eric's lack of discipline in such idyllic surroundings. He and his band together with Ronnie Wood moved on to the Band's Shangri-la Studios for the recording of their next album. Eric had always liked The Band since hearing their first album *Music From The Big Pink* back in 1968 when he was still with Cream, so it was quite a thrill to record with them at their studios overlooking the Pacific. It turned out that at some stage it had been a bordello with a colourful history attached to it.

During the early part of the sessions, Eric Clapton and Rick Danko went to Los Angeles to see the Crusaders who were playing at the Roxy. They were asked to come up and jam, but as it wasn't planned, their guitarist, Larry Carlton, had to lend Eric his Gibson ES335. They were also joined by Elton John and Stevie Wonder and a young Greg Phillinganes on the piano. A fun time was had by all.

The Shangri-la sessions featured a number of guests other than those already mentioned: Ronnie Wood, Robbie Robertson, Garth Hudson, Rick Danko, Richard Manuel, Jesse Ed Davis, Georgie Fame and Bob Dylan. The Dylan track was a song called 'Sign Language' in which Eric and Bob duetted on some lines. Half way through the sessions, Clapton held his birthday party at the studios and everything and everyone was recorded although it is unlikely ever to be released. Guests at the party all made contributions, Billy Preston singing various Ray Charles songs, Van Morrison singing 'Who Do You Love' and 'Stormy Monday', Rick Danko singing 'Hard Times' and Bob Dylan singing Beatle songs. Eric played guitar throughout and took occasional vocals as well as a duet on a little ditty with Billy Preston entitled 'It's Eric Clapton's Birthday'. Everyone enjoyed in hugely, even if they did not remember most of it the next day.

By the end of the sessions in April 1976 around 25 tracks had been completed. Clapton had also found time to guest on other people's sessions including one with Joe Cocker on a song called 'Worrier', with Ringo Starr on a number written by Eric called 'Could This Be Called A Song' which had originally been recorded at Shangri-la, and with Stephen Bishop on the tracks 'Save It For A Rainy Day' and 'Sinking In An Ocean Of Tears'. He also played on a Van Morrison session along with the The Crusaders, but this has never been released.

The Shangri-la sessions resulted in the *No Reason To Cry* album which was released in August. Among

Left: The 1975 tours were the ones, Eric buffs will recall, when the guitar hero took to wearing a beret for a while

Below: Relaxing during the 1976 sessions at the Shangri La Studios in Malibu, California

■ SET LIST ■
U.K. tour 1976
Set list taken from the following and would differ nightly:

Hello Old Friend • All Our Past Times • I Shot The Sheriff • Tell The Truth • Nobody Loves You When You're Down And Out • Kansas City • Stormy Monday • Going Down Slow • Badge • Double Trouble • Innocent Times • Can't Find My Way

SEASIDE ROCK!

Fans invade the lake in front of the stage at London's Crystal Palace Bowl

To promote the album's release, Clapton did his first full U.K. tour since Derek and the Dominos back in 1970. Being summer, it was decided to concentrate on seaside resorts to make it more fun for the band. They spent two days rehearsing at Shepperton Studios before playing a low key show at The Pavilion in Hemel Hempstead and then moving on to London's open-air Crystal Palace Bowl.

The shows opened with two acoustic numbers from the new album, 'Hello Old Friend' and 'All Our Pastimes' before progressing to the electric part of the set. Similar to previous tours, the running order and context would differ nightly. At the London show Larry Coryell joined Clapton for 'Going Down Slow' and 'Stormy Monday' as well as the final encore of 'Further On Up The Road' which also featured Ronnie Wood and Freddie King on guitars with all five guitarists taking turns to solo. The show was quite short at 80 minutes, mainly due to the constant flood of fans jumping into the lake situated at the foot of the stage. The lake created not only a security risk but endangered the band with the possibility of electrocution from the massive amount of wiring required for the sound system.

Van Morrison also put in a couple of appearances with Eric, singing on spirited versions of 'Kansas City' and 'Stormy Monday'. One of these shows at the Birmingham Odeon resulted in an unfortunate outburst in which Clapton jokingly stated that he would be standing for parliament and that Enoch Powell, a politician known for his strong views against minority immigration, should be Prime Minister. The press reacted strongly, accusing the guitarist of being racist — a great irony in the face of his close affiliation to black music and musicians. Although he was drunk when the words came out of his mouth, the incident also exposed the degree of Eric's political naivety. However, it was something that was held against him for a long time and was a direct stimulus for the formation of the organization 'Rock Against Racism'.

The tour continued without further incident and the last date on 17 August was held at Warners

its highlights was a version of Otis Rush's 'Double Trouble', which was to become a stage favourite during the coming years, giving him ample opportunity to show his skill as a master blues guitarist, and Bob Dylan's 'Sign Language', a duet with Bob featuring a Robbie Robertson guitar solo and Clapton on dobro and acoustic guitar.

On his return to England, Clapton once again joined the Rolling Stones on stage, this time at Granby Halls in Leicester for 'Brown Sugar' and 'Key To The Highway'.

Holiday Camp in Hayling Island: an odd choice as holiday camps in England are renowned as places where families can enjoy their holidays at low cost. They are not the ideal venue for a rock concert. The daily entertainments organized by the camp representatives were more likely to include 'knobbly knees' contests and bingo games! Surprisingly, Clapton felt quite comfortable playing to a crowd to whom rock concerts were a novelty. He lightened the mood by changing the titles of songs to suit his audience, such as 'Nobody Knows You When You're In Hayling Island'. His sense of humour and adaptability paid off. By the time he reached the encore, 'Key To The Highway', couples young and old were swinging on the dance floor.

Eric and Pattie stayed on at home in England after the tour and attended a Buddy Holly luncheon organized by Paul McCartney on 7 September, an event notable for the fact that Clapton wrote a song entitled 'You Look Wonderful Tonight' after the function. He recorded it as a demo with his friend Ronnie Lane a few days later. Little did he realize what impact the song would have on young lovers everywhere, when the song was re-recorded in May

1977 and released as a single shortened to 'Wonderful Tonight'. Along with 'Layla', it is one of Clapton's most requested songs and remains a firm favourite at all his shows.

One of Eric's influences at this time was American country singer Don Williams, whose work revealed a gentle side to country music which was not always apparent in the genre. He joined Williams on stage at London's Hammersmith Odeon in September to play some exquisite dobro and was later to record one of his songs for his next album. He also introduced Pete Townshend and Ronnie Lane to Don at the show.

A 13-date American tour started on 5 November at the Bay Front Center in St Petersburg, Florida. One of the shows at the Dallas Convention Centre was recorded and highlights broadcast on the radio. Freddie King joined in for 'Further On Up The Road' at the show.

After this tour Clapton went to San Francisco to attend rehearsals with his friends the Band, who were ending life on the road after some 16 years with a spectacular concert at the Winterland on 26 November. They called the show 'The Last Waltz' and invited everyone that had been involved with them during

A pint of beer backstage at the Crystal Palace gig

The Crystal Palace concert proved another triumph for Clapton in front of his London fans

their career: a star-studded cast included Bob Dylan, Van Morrison, Dr. John, Neil Young, Joni Mitchell, Ronnie Hawkins, Muddy Waters and Neil Diamond. Eric Clapton played on 'All Our Pastimes' and 'Further On Up The Road' which featured some amazing guitar duelling between him and Robbie Robertson. He also joined in the all-star finale of 'I Shall Be Released' and was carried back on stage by Bill Graham for some instumental jams with Ronnie Wood, Carl Radle, Neil Young, Robbie Robertson, Paul Butterfield and Levon Helm. The show was filmed by Martin Scorsese and recorded by the Wally Heider Mobile and has become a classic of live rock on film.

SLOWHAND

*E*ric Clapton had been seeing a lot of Ronnie Lane over the previous few months, both at his home and Ronnie's place in Wales. Clapton's first live appearance in 1977 was a

secret charity show on St. Valentine's Day at Cranleigh village hall, involving Ronnie's band Slim Chance. The posters were advertising an evening with Eddie And The Earth Tremors with special guests. The audience numbered 350 and were treated to Eric on guitar and vocals with Ronnie Lane on guitar and vocals, Bruce Rowland on drums, Charlie Hart on keyboards and accordion and Brian Belshaw on bass, playing a set that included 'How Come', 'Willie And The Hand Jive', 'Alberta' and 'Goodnight Irene'.

Clapton was very much into playing small anonymous venues, and virtually impromptu sessions would often occur at Gary Brooker's pub, the Parrot Inn, near Eric's house. In late February he also played on a session for Pete Townshend and Ronnie Lane at Olympic Studios in Barnes. Glyn Johns produced the sessions, which gave him an opportunity of getting to know the guitarist. They had met him a few times before at various guest sessions, but Clapton would normally be on the defensive in a studio full of strangers and consequently gave the wrong impression of being rude. However, over the course of the week they became good friends and Clapton asked Johns to produce his upcoming album. Glyn is and

Eric at the beginning of yet another American tour, towards the end of 1976

was a well respected producer who has worked with the Beatles, the Who, the Rolling Stones, Joan Armatrading, Leon Russell and Marc Benno to name but a few.

On 20 April 1977, Eric and his band started an eight date UK tour at the De Montfort Hall in Leicester. On 26 April they filmed an 'Old Grey Whistle Test' television special for the B.B.C. which was for later broadcast before playing two shows at Hammersmith Odeon. They were recorded by the Ronnie Lane Mobile for a possible double live album. The shows started with three acoustic numbers 'Hello Old Friend', 'Sign Language' and 'Alberta' followed by the electric part of the set, a highlight of which was a lengthy version of the blues classic 'Stormy Monday', a number that has yet to appear on a Clapton album.

The last date of the tour was at the Rainbow in London, scene of Eric's comeback concerts, where he was joined onstage by Pete Townshend for some power chords on 'Layla' and 'Crossroads'. A few days later Eric and his band went to Olympic Studios for the recording of their next album, *Slowhand*. As mentioned earlier, Clapton at last got to record 'Wonderful Tonight'. Other tracks recorded included 'The Riff', which became 'Burning Hot Core' and was finally shortened to 'The Core'. This featured sax by Mel Collins and a powerful solo by Eric, centred around a basic riff, hence the original title. Also recorded were 'Alberta' which had been previewed

on the tour, J.J. Cale's 'Cocaine', Don Williams' 'We're All The Way', Arthur Crudup's 'Mean Old Frisco', a version of which had been recorded earlier during the aborted second Derek And The Dominos album sessions, and John Martyn's 'May You Never'. Eric and Pattie organized the cover for *Slowhand*, and designed the inner gatefold spread.

Four days after the sessions ended, another tour started in Ireland before moving on to Scandinavia and Europe. No new songs were performed, mainly due to the fact that there had been no time to rehearse them. A novel aspect of this tour was travelling by train to get from country to country. They rented three luxury coaches in Germany, including the dining car from the Orient Express, and had them coupled to the end of the appropriate train heading for the next location on the tour. Ronnie Lane's Slim Chance were once again the support act and both he and Clapton would often busk on various station platforms totally unrecognized and taking a fair amount of foreign coinage in the process.

After the shows they would return to the train for a good old fashion sing-song to such tunes as 'Maybe It's Because I'm A Londoner' and 'My Old Man Says Follow The Van'. Eric had shaved off his beard but had kept his moustache, giving him the look of a country and western singer rather than that of a rock guitarist. The shows were enjoyed by everyone and in Brussels, a member of the rather boisterous audience kept shouting out for 'Bell Bottom Blues'. Clapton proceeded to introduce each number as this much-requested classic before launching into something completely different!

One of the highlights of the whole tour was a lengthy version of 'I Shot The Sheriff' with some incredible wah wah guitar work. In Paris, the fans had a special surprise when Ringo Starr appeared on stage with tambourine in hand during 'Badge'. After the final show in Munich on 20 June everyone travelled back to England before heading off to Spain for a further two concerts.

Just before this Ronnie Lane together with Eric Clapton and his old band mate from the Roosters, Tom McGuinness, played an amazing show at the Drum And Monkey pub in Shropshire, Ronnie's local at the time. Holding it in the car park on a hot summer evening set off the mood perfectly. The band also featured Ian Stewart, from the Rolling Stones, on

keyboards, Charlie Hart on fiddle, Jim Jewel on sax and an unknown rhythm section. Numbers performed included a version of the Stones's 'Dead Flowers' followed by 'Willie And The Hand Jive', 'Singing The Blues', 'Walk On By', 'Da Doo Ron Ron', 'Ooh La La', 'Key To The Highway', 'Little Queenie', 'Goodnight Irene', and a lengthy version of 'Stormy Monday' giving Clapton ample opportunity to demonstrate his skills with some scorching lead guitar work. The three-hour show ended with a version of Dylan's 'If You Gotta Go'. Probably the best pub band in the world!

On 1 August, he chartered *The Welsh Liberty*, a sleek steel-hulled yacht, that would take him and the band from Cannes to Ibiza for a concert at the Bull Ring before moving on to the mainland at the Nuevo Pabellon Club in Barcelona. The show in Ibiza left a lot to be desired, the acoustics were terrible due to the concrete surroundings and the backstage area was

Sittin' this one out . . . Eric onstage during a soundcheck on the 1978 U.S. tour

situated in the rooms where injured matadors were operated on. Not exactly conducive for a good rock'n'-roll atmosphere. The yacht sailed back to Cannes on 12 August.

In late September they set off on another Japanese tour commencing at the Festival Hall in Osaka. This was the first opportunity to perform some of the new material that had been recorded back in May. 'The Core' live was even more powerful than its studio version and would open the shows rather than the acoustic numbers that had started the concerts in all previous tours since 1974. The acoustic material was performed in the middle of the set and comprised 'Alberta', 'Sign Language' and 'We're All The Way'. As always, they were very well received in Japan. Two more shows followed in Honolulu, Hawaii before coming home.

The May sessions had resulted in the *Slowhand* album, containing the future concert favourites 'Wonderful Tonight', 'Cocaine' and 'Lay Down Sally', released in November to critical acclaim, not to mention huge sales. Finally, in December, Clapton along with Stevie Winwood played on sessions for Island artist Ijahman Levi at Joe Gibbs' studio.

ROLLING HOTEL

Clapton started the year with yet another recording session, this time at Olympic Studios in Barnes, London, for a forthcoming album about the American Civil War called *White Mansions*. He played only on two numbers, entitled 'White Trash' on which he used electic slide, and 'Kentucky Racehorse', using dobro. Other artists on the session were Tim Hinkley, Henry Spinetti, Dave Markee, Steve Cash, Jimi Colter, Bernie Leadon, Paul Kennerly and John Dillon.

A huge North American tour to promote *Slowhand* kicked off on 1 February at the P.N.E. Coliseum in Vancouver, Canada. He even had a hit in the American country charts with 'Lay Down Sally' and would regularly appear on stage in a cowboy hat. The country influence was also reflected in the numbers performed, including 'Rodeo Man', 'We're All The Way' and 'Next Time You See Her'. The set of course

did include the usual crowd pleasers like 'Layla', 'Let It Rain', 'Badge', 'Cocaine' and 'Bottle Of Red Wine', along with a pleasant surprise called 'Fools Paradise' by Buddy Holly.

The first part of the tour ended on 2 March at the Boutwell Auditorium in Birmingham, Alabama. During the following two-week break, Clapton returned home to indulge his other passion, soccer. He supported West Bromwich Albion and went to see them knock Nottingham Forest out of the F.A. Cup competition on 11 March.

Above: *The Nassau Coliseum, Long Island, was a regular stop on Clapton's many tours of America*

Left: *Surrounded by guitars, amplifiers and monitor speakers, there was not much room for manoeuvre*

■ SET LIST ■

Set list was taken from the following and would differ nightly:

Peaches And Diesel • Wonderful Tonight • Lay Down Sally • Next Time You See Her • Mean Old Frisco • The Core • All The Way • Rodeo Man • Fools Paradise • Cocaine • Badge • Let It Rain • Knockin' On Heaven's Door • Key To The Highway • Going Down Slow • Layla • Bottle Of Red Wine • You'll Never Walk Alone • Further On Up The Road

He returned to America for the second part of the tour starting at the Jai-Alai Fronton in Miami on 19 March and ending on 9 April at the Maple Leaf Gardens in Toronto, Canada. Part of a show recorded at the Civic Auditorium, Santa Monica was broadcast on 26 March on the 'King Biscuit Flower Hour Radio Show'. A couple of weeks after his return, Eric joined

plus shows he had been performing in the United States. Dylan gave Clapton a cassette of two unreleased songs to record for his next album: 'Walk Out In The Rain' and 'If I Don't Be There By Morning'.

In fact, sessions had already started in late May at Olympic Studios in Barnes and would continue at regular intervals until September. One of the first tracks to be recorded was 'Tulsa Time' written by Don Williams's guitarist, Danny Flowers. Other tracks included J.J. Cale's 'I'll Make Love To You Anytime', 'Watch Out For Lucy', 'Tell Me That You Love Me', 'Golden Ring', 'Promises', 'It's A Shame', 'Early In The Morning', 'Roll It', 'Sweet Lorraine', 'The Road Is Long', 'Depend On Me' and 'Before You Accuse Me'. Quite a few instrumental jams were also recorded. Don Williams' influence could still be felt, particularly on Clapton's composition 'Golden Ring'.

The new album came out in November and was titled *Backless* which related to Dylan at Blackbushe where he was very aware of what was going on behind them both on and off stage. After the sessions, George Terry left to resume session work and Marcy Levy left to pursue a solo career.

The usual promotional tour started in Spain on 5 November at the Pabellon Deportivo Del Real Madrid in the Spanish capital and progressed through Europe and England including a show at the Gala Ballroom, West Bromwich, home of his favourite football team. The train was again used for the European portion of the tour and filmed by Rex Pyke who was making a documentary about Clapton. A show at the Glasgow Apollo was recorded and filmed by him with the guitarist performing Robert Johnson's 'Kindhearted Woman Blues', possibly the only time he performed the song in concert. Another highlight of the tour was Eric's hometown gig at Guildford's Civic Hall, which was also filmed, featuring Elton John and George Harrison on the encore of 'Further On Up The Road'. The resultant film, *Eric Clapton And His Rolling Hotel* has rarely been seen, no doubt due in part to the fact that it shows Clapton at a time when he was drinking fairly heavily.

The musical running order for the tour was different every night. 'Tulsa Time' segued into 'Early In The Morning', both featuring some inspired slide guitar work, and 'Cocaine' with an extended guitar solo. The shows differed in length from as little as 80 minutes in Brussels to almost 120 minutes in Glasgow.

Eric joined an impromptu band on the occasion of the wedding of Glyn Johns, who had produced Eric's albums Slowhand *and* Backless *for him*

Alexis Korner on stage at the Gatsby Room, Pinewood Studios, alongside Colin Hodgkinson on bass, Zoot Money on electric piano, Stu Speer on drums, Dick Morrissey, Dick Heckstall-Smith, Art Themen, Mel Collins, John Surman on saxes, Mike Zwerim on trombone, Chris Farlowe on vocals, Duffy Power on harmonica, Paul Jones on harmonica and Neil Ford on guitar. Eric played on 'Hey Pretty Mama', 'Can't Get You Out Of My Mind', 'High Heel Sneakers', and 'Stormy Monday Blues'. The event was to celebrate Alexis Korner's 50th birthday and was filmed and recorded by the B.B.C. for later broadcast.

In May, it was announced that Clapton was to play three major festivals with Bob Dylan headlining. They were held at Feÿenourd Stadium, Rotterdam on 23 June, the Zeppelin Field in Nuremburg on 1 July and lastly at Blackbushe Aerodrome in Hampshire on 15 July. In Nuremburg, Eric joined Dylan for 'I'll Be Your Baby Tonight' and 'The Times They Are A Changin'. He also joined him at Blackbushe for 'Forever Young'. Clapton's own sets lasted 90 minutes in this festival situation, compared to the two-hour-

The London dates were at the Hammersmith Odeon, the shows opening with a version of Clapton's favourite Stevie Wonder song, 'Loving You Is Sweeter Than Ever'. Muddy Waters and his band were the support on the tour and occasionally joined Eric for a jam, much to the delight of the audience. At the end of the tour, Clapton returned the compliment and joined Muddy onstage at Dingwalls in London's Camden Town for a lengthy session of blues. It was a rare moment for music lovers to see the two giants playing together in a club environment.

At the end of December 1978 Eric and his band went to Olympic Studios to record some tracks which to this day remain unreleased. They were 'Water On The Ground', 'To Make Somebody Happy' and 'Cryin'.

WONDERFUL TONIGHT?

*I*n early 1979 Eric Clapton along with Albert Lee, Dick Sims, Jim Keltner, Carl Radle and Dick Morresey played on a session for Marc Benno at Olympic Studios in Barnes.

The whole thing was produced by Glyn Johns who had worked with Benno back in the early 1970s on previous solo albums.

Albert Lee joined Clapton's band in January at manager Roger Forrester's suggestion to give him a fuller sound in concert. Lee had a thoroughbred background having played with Chris Farlowe and the Thunderbirds, Head Hands and Feet, and Emmylou Harris' Hot Band, not to mention countless sessions over the years. His style was different to Eric's, and the resulting union was a pleasure to see and hear.

Rehearsals for a forthcoming Irish and American tour took place from 20 February to 3 March inclusive. The eight-date Irish tour started at the City Hall in Cork on 8 March and ended at Dublin's National Stadium on 17 March. Numbers played included 'Watch Out For Lucy' performed for the first time, as well as Mark Knopfler's 'Setting Me Up' which was Albert's solo spot. The remainder of the set was the same as the four piece band's European and English tour. For the American leg, Muddy Waters played support. The first part was ended at the Spectrum in Philadelphia on 30 April.

On 27 March, the eve of the American tour, Eric

Eric at home with Patti, soon to be his wife, on what were at the time rare occasions that they could relax together . . . and even then, someone had to take a photograph!

Clapton finally married Patti Boyd in Tucson, Arizona. There had been many ups and downs during their relationship, but at last they were wed at the Apostolic Assembly of Faith in Christ Jesus. The next night, at the first show, in Tucson's Community Center, Eric brought Patti out onstage so he could sing 'Wonderful Tonight' to her in front of a mesmerized audience.

By the end of April, Patti was already back in England and when her husband returned, he found that a huge wedding celebration party had been organized in the garden of his country home for family and friends. A stage was set up in a marquee where historic jams with Paul McCartney, George Harrison and Ringo Starr as well as Lonnie Donegan and Jack Bruce took place. Needless to say, security was extremely tight. It was later learned that John Lennon, who was in America at the time, would have flown over had he known about it! It was the closest the Beatles ever came to performing together again.

The second leg of the U.S. tour started on the 25 May at the Civic Center in Augusta, Maine. On 12 June at the Stadium in Chicago, Clapton joined Muddy Waters and Willie Dixon for 'Got My Mojo Working'. Muddy later joined Clapton with Johnny Winter for 'Kansas City' and 'Long Distance Call'. On a rare day off, on 17 June in Omaha, Clapton met

Roger McGuinn in the lobby of the Hilton Hotel where they were both staying with their respective bands. McGuinn invited Clapton to jam that night with himself, Clark, and Hillman, resulting in a wonderful version of the Byrds' classic 'Eight Miles High' featuring some great guitar duelling between Eric and Roger. Clapton asked him to return the compliment the following night at the Civic Auditorium for a version of 'Knockin' On Heaven's Door'. According to reports, McGuinn sang a rare verse Dylan had written but not recorded on the original version.

The American tour finished at the Coliseum in Seattle, Washington on 24 June. Now Clapton decided it was time for a change, dispensing with Dick Sims, Jamie Oldaker and Carl Radle but keeping Albert Lee. Although he had always been more enthusiastic about American musicians, Clapton decided to go for an all-British band to bring a new lease of life to his sound. Drummer Henry Spinetti, bassist Dave Markee and Chris Stainton on keyboards were brought in to replace them. Henry and Dave were probably the best rhythm section around at that time having contributed solid backing on a variety of sessions that included albums by Joan Armatrading, Leo Sayer and Andy Fairweather-Low. They had also played with Clapton earlier on both the Pete Townshend/Ronnie Lane and *White Mansions* albums.

The new all-British band made a low key debut at Cranleigh village hall on 7 September and at the Victoria Hall in Hanley on 30 September before embarking on a tour that would take them to Austria, Germany, Yugoslavia, Poland, Israel, Thailand, The Philippines, Hong Kong and Japan. Although Eric had been drinking steadily since 1974, it was not until this period that drink started seriously to affect his performance. Listening to tapes of shows from this time, it is clear that while alcohol caused no obvious harm to his guitar playing, his vocals began to sound rough — although this seemed eminently suitable for the blues numbers. He wasn't letting the audience down, but he was well on the way to killing himself.

The tour went well, particularly in places like Israel, Bangkok and Hong Kong where Clapton had not played before. However, the Polish dates ended in disaster. Back in 1979, this was still a country very much under authoritarian rule. Two concerts at the Sala Kongresso in Warsaw had gone by without incident. But the next evening's concert at the Hala

Sportowo in Katowice proved traumatic for Clapton. As fans rushed the stage to get a better view, the security guards forcibly removed them, spraying them with tear gas. House lights were turned on to reveal a row of security guards with truncheons at the ready should anyone else get out of their seat. Eric was totally powerless because of the language barrier. No encore was performed and the next night's concert was cancelled at the last moment as the Polish authorities refused to comply with Roger Forrester's security instructions. The fans who were already in the hall rioted, causing serious damage to the sound system, replacements being flown to Israel, the next stop.

Almost at the end of this tour, at Tokyo's Budokan, two shows were recorded for a live double album which very faithfully reproduced the sound of the band. Listening to *Just One Night* now, this does show up the weaknesses of the group, who although they were great musicians, did not seem to have the same feel as Eric for the spontaneity that was needed to keep things alive and kicking.

DISCOGRAPHY

SINGLES
I Shot The Sheriff (*Marley*)
Give Me Strength (*Clapton*)
U.K. RSO 2090132/U.S. RSO 409
Criteria Studios, Miami
April/May 1974
Prod. Tom Dowd
Released July 1974

Willie And The Hand Jive (*Otis*)
Mainline Florida (*Terry*)
U.K. RSO 2090139/U.S. RSO 503
Criteria Studios, Miami
Prod. Tom Dowd
Released October 1974

Swing Low Sweet Chariot (*trad. arr. Clapton*)

Pretty Blue Eyes (*Clapton*)
U.K. RSO 2090158
Dynamic Sound Studios,
Kingston, Jamaica
August 1974
Prod. Tom Dowd
Released May 1975

Knocking On Heaven's Door
(*Dylan*)
Someone Like You (*Louis*)
U.K. RSO 2090166
Criteria Studios, Miami
16th June 1975
Prod. Tom Dowd, Albhy Galuten
Released August 1975

Hello Old Friend (*Clapton*)
All Our Pastimes (*Clapton, Danko*)
U.K. RSO 2090208/U.S. RSO 861
Shangri La Studios, Malibu,
California
March/April 1976
Prod. Rob Fraboni
Released October 1976

Carnival (*Clapton*)
Hungry (*Sims, Levy*)
U.K. RSO 2090222
Shangri La Studios, Malibu,
California
March/April 1976
Prod. Rob Fraboni
Released February 1977

Lay Down Sally (*Levy, Clapton*)
Cocaine (*Cale*)
U.K. RSO 2090264
Olympic Studios, London
May 1977
Prod. Glyn Johns
Released November 1977

Wonderful Tonight (*Clapton*)

Peaches And Diesel (*Galuten, Clapton*)
U.K. RSO 2090275/U.S. RSO 895
Olympic Studios, London
May 1977
Prod. Glyn Johns
Released March 1978

Promises (*Feldman, Linn*)
Watch Out For Lucy (*Clapton*)
U.K. RSO 21/ U.S. RSO 910
Olympic Studios, London
May–Sept 1978
Prod. Glyn Johns
Released October 1978

If I Don't Be There By Morning
(*Dylan*)
Tulsa Time (*Flowers*)
U.K. RSO 24
Olympic Studios, London
May–Sept 1978
Prod. Glyn Johns
Released March 1979

ALBUMS
461 OCEAN BOULEVARD
Motherless Chldren (*trad. arr. Clapton*), **Give Me Strength** (*Clapton*), **Willie And The Hand Jive** (*Otis*), **Get Ready** (*Clapton, Elman*), **I Shot The Sheriff** (*Marley*), **I Can't Hold Out Much Longer** (*James*), **Please Be With Me** (*Scott-Boyer*), **Let It Grow** (*Clapton*), **Steady Rollin' May** (*Johnson*), **Mainline Florida** (*Terry*).
U.K. RSO 2479118/ U.S. RSO SO 4801
Criteria Studios, Miami
April–May 1974
Prod. Tom Dowd
Released August 1974

THERE'S ONE IN EVERY CROWD
We've Been Told (*Jesus Coming Soon*), (*Johnson arr. Clapton*), **Swing Low Sweet Chariot** (*trad. arr. Clapton*), **Little Rachel** (*Byfield*), **Don't Blame Me** (*Clapton, Terry*), **The Sky Is Crying** (*James, Robinson*), **Singin' The Blues** (*McCreary*), **Better Make It Through Today** (*Clapton*), **Pretty Blue Eyes**

(Clapton), **High** (Clapton), **Opposites** (Clapton),
U.K. RSO 2479132/ U.S. RSO SO4806
Dynamic Sounds Studio, Kingston, Jamaica
August–September 1974
Prod. Tom Dowd
Released April 1975

E.C. WAS HERE
Have You Ever Loved A Woman? (*Myles*), **Presence Of The Lord** (*Clapton*), **Drifting Blues** (*Moore, Brown, Williams*), **Can't Find My Way Home** (*Winwood*), **Rambling On My Mind** (*trad. arr. Clapton*), **Further On Up The Road** (*Veasey, Robey*),
U.K. RSO 2394160/ U.S. RSO SO 4809
Live recordings at Long Beach Arena, Florida (19, 20th July 1974), Hammersmith Odeon, London (4th December 1974)
Prod. Tom Dowd
Released August 1975

NO REASON TO CRY
Beautiful Thing (*Manuel, Danko*), **Carnival** (*Clapton*), **Sign Language** (*Dylan*), **County Jail Blues** (*Fields*), **All Our Past Times** (*Clapton, Danko*), **Hello Old Friend** (*Clapton*), **Double Trouble** (*Rush*), **Innocent Times** (*Clapton, Levy*), **Hungry** (*Sims, Levy*), **Black Summer** (*Clapton*),
U.K. RSO 2394160/ U.S. RSO 1-3004
Shangri La Studios, Malibu, California
February–April 1976
Prod. Rob Fraboni
Released August 1976

SLOWHAND
Cocaine (*Cale*), **Wonderful Tonight** (*Clapton*), **Lay Down Sally** (*Levy, Clapton*), **We're All The Way** (*Williams*), **The Core** (*Levy, Clapton*), **May You Never** (*Martyn*), **Mean Old Frisco** (*trad.*), **Peaches And Diesel** (*Galuten, Clapton*),
U.K. RSO 2479201/ U.S. RSO RS 1-3030
Olympic Studios, London
May 1977

Prod. Glyn Johns
Released November 1977

BACKLESS
Walk Out In The Rain (*Dylan*), **Watch Out For Lucy** (*Clapton*), **I'll Make Love To You** (*Cale*), **Roll It** (*Levy, Clapton*), **Tell Me That You Love Me** (*Clapton*), **If I Don't Be There By Morning** (*Dylan*), **Early In The Morning** (*arr. Clapton*), **Promises** (*Feldman, Linn*), **Golden Ring** (*Clapton*), **Tulsa Time** (*Flowers*),
U.K. RSO 5001/ U.S. RSO RS 1-3039
Olympic Studios, London
May–September 1978
Prod. Glyn Johns
Released November 1978

■ TOURS ■

1974
June
20th Tivoli Gdns, Stockholm
21st KB Halle, Copenhagen
U.S.A. TOUR
28th Yale Bowl, Newhaven, Conneticut **29th** Spectrum, Philadelphia **30th** Nasau Coliseum, Long Island
July
2nd International Amphitheatre, Chicago **4th** Music Park, Columbus, Ohio **5th** Three River Stadium, Pittsburgh **6th** Buffalo Bill Stadium, Buffalo, NY **7th** Roosevelt Stadium, Jersey City, NJ **9th** Montreal Forum **10th** Civic Centre, Providence Rhode Island **12th** Boston Cardens, Boston, Massachusetts **13th** Madison Square Garden, NYC **14th** Capitol Centre, Largo, Maryland **18th** Diablo Stadium, Tempe, Arizona **19th/20th** Long Beach Arena, Long Beach, California **21st** Cow Palace, San Francisco **23rd** Denver Coliseum, Denver, Colorado **25th** Neil Auditorium, St Louis, Missouri **27th** Mississippi Valley Fairgrounds, Davenport, Iowa **28th** Memphis Memorial Stadium, Memphis, Tennessee **29th** Legion Field, Birmingham, Alabama **31st** City Park Stadium, New Orleans

August
1st The Omni, Atlanta, Georgia
2nd Coliseum, Greensborough, North Carolina **4th** West Palm Beach Raceway, Florida
September
28th Hampton Roads Coliseum, Virginia
29th Nassau Coliseum, Long Island NY
30th Boston Gardens, Boston, Massachusetts
October
1st Montreal Forum **2nd** Maple Leaf Gardens, Toronto **4th/5th** Capitol Center, Largo, Maryland **6th** Spectrum, Philadelphia

JAPAN TOUR 1974
October
31st Budokan, Tokyo
November
1st/2nd Budokan, Tokyo
5th/6th Hoseinenkin Hall, Osaka

EUROPE TOUR
November
26th Congress Centrum, Hamburg **27th** Olympic Hall, Munich **28th** Friedrich-Ebert Halle, Ludwigshaven **29th** Grugahalle, Essen **30th** Ahoy Hall, Rotterdam
December
1st Sport Palais, Antwerp
2nd Parc Des Expositions, Paris
4th/5th Hammersmith Odeon, London

1975
HAWAII/AUSTRALASIA
April
7th/8th Hic Arena, Honolulu, Hawaii 11th Western Springs, Auckland New Zealand 13th/14th Festival Hall, Melbourne 17th/19th Horden Pavilion, Sydney 23rd Festival Hall, Brisbane 26th Memorial Park Drive, Adelaide 28th Entertainments Centre, Perth

U.S.A TOUR
June
14th Tampa Stadium, Tampa, Florida 15th Jacksonville Coliseum, Jacksonville, Florida 17th Mobile Muncipal Auditorium, Mobile, Alabama 18th Mid-South Coliseum, Memphis, Tennessee 19th Knoxville Coliseum, Knoxville, Tennessee 20th Charlotte Coliseum, Charlotte, North Carolina 21st, Cincinatti Gardens, Cincinatti, Ohio 23rd Niagara Convention Center, Niagara, New York 24th Civic Center, Springfield, Massachusetts 25th Providence Civic Center, Providence, Rhode Island 26th Saratoga Performing Arts Centre, Saratoga, New York 28th Nassau Coliseum, Uniondale, New York 29th Civic Center, New Haven, Connecticut 30th Civic Center, Pittsburgh, Pennsylvania
July
1st Olympia Stadium, Detroit, Michigan 3rd Baltimore Stadium, Baltimore, Maryland 4th Richfield Coliseum, Cleveland Ohio 5th Chicago Stadium, Illinois 7th Met Sports Center, Minneapolis, Minnesota 8th Dane County Coliseum, Madison, Wisconsin 10th Municipal Auditorium, Kansas City, Missouri 11th Kiel Auditorium, St. Louis, Missouri

August
3rd PNE Coliseum, Vancouver, British Columbia 4th Coliseum, Portland Oregon 5th Coliseum, Seattle, Washington 6th Coliseum, Spokane, Washington 9th Stanford University, Stanford California 11th Salt Palace, Salt Lake City, Utah 12th Coliseum, Denver, Colorado 14th The Forum, Los Angeles, California 15th Swing Auditorium, San Bernardino, California 16th Sports Arena, San Diego, California 17th Community Center, Tuscon, Arizona 18th Civic Center, El Paso, Texas 20th Sam Houston Coliseum, Houston, Texas 21st Tarrant Convention Centre, Fort Worth Texas 22nd Myriad Coliseum, Oklahoma City, Oklahoma 23rd Assembly Center, Tulsa, Oklahoma 24th Hirsh Coliseum, Shreveport, Louisiana 27th Market Square Arena, Indianapolis, Indiana 28th Municipal Auditorium, Charleston, South Carolina 29th Coliseum, Greensboro, North Carolina 30th The Scope, Norfolk, Virginia

JAPAN TOUR
October
22nd Festival Hall, Osaka 23rd Festival Hall, Osaka 24th Kyoto Kaikan Hall, Kyoto 27th Kokura Sogo Taikukan, Fukuoka 29th Sumpu Kaikan, Shizuoka
November
1st Budokan, Tokyo
2nd Budokan, Tokyo

1976
BRITISH TOUR
July
29th The Pavilion, Marlowes, Hemel Hempstead
31st Crystal Palace Bowl, London
August
1st The Gaumont Theatre, Southampton, Hants 2nd Town Hall, Torquay, Devon 3rd A.B C., Plymouth Devon 5th Odeon Theatre, New Street, Birmingham 6th Belle Vue, Hyde Road, Manchester 7th Lancaster University, Lancaster 9th Apollo Centre, Glasgow, Scotland 10th Apollo Centre, Glasgow, Scotland 12th City Hall, Newcastle-Upon-

Tyne 13th The Spa, Bridlington, Yorkshire 15th A.B.C., Church Street, Blackpool 17th Pontins Holiday Camp, Camber Sands, Sussex

U.S.A. TOUR
November
5th Bay Front Centre, St. Petersburg, Florida 6th Sportatorium, Miami, Florida 7th The Coliseum, Jacksonville, Florida 9th The Omni Theatre, Atlanta, Georgia 10th Municipal Auditorium, Mobile, Alabama 11th The Assembly Center, Baton Rouge, Louisiana 13th Hofeinz Pavilion, Houston, Texas 14th Convention Center, Dallas, Texas 16th The Lloyd Noble Center, Norman, Oklahoma 18th PAN AM Center, Las Cruces, New Mexico 19th The Coliseum, Phoenix, Arizona 20th Sports Auditorium, San Diego, California 22nd The Forum, Los Angeles, California

1977
February
14th Village Hall, Cranleigh

BRITISH TOUR
April
20th De Montfort Hall, Leicester 21st Belle Vue, Manchester 22nd Victoria Hall, Stoke 23rd Apollo Centre, Glasgow 24th City Hall, Newcastle Upon Tyne 26th "Old Grey Whistle Test" T.V. Special, London 27th/28th The Odeon, Hammersmith London 29th Rainbow Theatre, London

EUROPEAN TOUR
June
4th/6th National Stadium, Dublin, Eire 9th Falkoner Theatre, Copenhagen, Denmark 10th Stadthalle, Bremen, Germany 11th Groenoordhalle, Leiden, Holland 13th Forest National, Brussels, Belgium 14th Le Pavillion, Paris, France 15th Philipshalle, Dusseldorf, Germany 17th Rhein Neckerhalle, Heidleberg, Germany 19th Mehrzweckhalle, Wiztzikon, Zurich, Switzerland 20th Olympia Halle, Munich, Germany

JAPAN TOUR
September
26th Festival Hall, Osaka **27th** Ken Taiiku-Kan, Okayama **29th** Kaikan Hall, Kyoto **30th** Shi Kokaido, Nagoya
October
1st, Festival Hall, Osaka **4th** Makima-Nai Ice Arena, Sapporo **6th/7th** Budokan, Tokyo **9th** International Center, Honolulu

---

1979
IRISH TOUR
March
8th City Hall, Cork **9th** St. John's Lyn's, Tralee **11th** Leisureland Galway **12th** Savoy Theatre, Limerick **13th** Stand Hill, Sligo **15th** Downtown Club, Dundalk **16th** Army Camp, Dublin **17th** National Stadium, Dublin

U.S.A. TOUR
28th Community Center, Tucson, Arizona **29th** Civic Center, Albuquerque, New Mexico **31st** U of TX Special Events Center, El Paso, Texas
April
1st Chapparral Center, Midland Texas **3rd** Lloyd Noble Center, Norman, Oklahoma **4th** Hammons Center, Springfield, Missouri **6th** Assembly Center, Tulsa, Oklahoma **7th** Convention Center, Pine Bluff, Arkansas **9th** Summit, Houston, Texas **10th** Tarrant Convention Center, Fort Worth Texas **11th** Municipal Auditorium, Austin, Texas **12th** Convention Center, San Antonio, Texas **14th** Civic Center, Monroe, Louisiana **15th** Municipal Auditorium, New Orleans, Louisana **17th** Freedom Hall, Johnson City, Tennessee **18th** Coliseum, Knoxville, Tennessee **20th** U of AL Coliseum, Tuscaloosa, Alabama **21st** Omni, Atlanta, Georgia **22nd** Municipal Auditorium, Mobile, Alabama **24th** William & Mary University, Williamsburg **25th** Mosque, Richmond Virginia **26th** Capitol Center, Washington D.C., Maryland **28th** Civic Center, Providence, Rhode Island **29th** Vet. Memorial Coliseum, New Haven,

Conneticut **30th** Spectrum, Philadelphia, Pennsylvania
May
25th Civic Center, Augusta, Maine **26th** Cumberland Co. Civic Center, Portland, Maryland **28th** Civic Center, Binghampton, New York State **29th** War Memorial Arena, Syracuse, New York State **30th** War Memorial, Rochester, New York State
June
1st Memorial Auditorium, Buffalo, New York State **2nd** Richfield Coliseum, Cleveland Ohio **4th** Sports Arena, Toledo, Ohio **5th** Civic Center, Saginaw, Michigan **7th** Riverfront Coliseum, Cincinnati, Ohio **8th** Market Square Arena, Indianapolis, Indiana **9th** Dane County Exposition Center, Madison, **10th** Civic Center, St. Paul, Minnesota

EUROPEAN TOUR
October
6th Stadthalle, Vienna, Austria **7th** Sporthalle, Linz, Austria **8th** Messehalle, Nurenberg, West Germany **10th** Palata Ioneer Hall, Belgrde, Yugoslavia **11th/12th** Dom Sportover, Zagreb, Yugoslavia **15th/16th** Sala Kongresso, Warsaw, Poland **17th/18th** Hala Sportowo, Kattowice, Poland
21st–25th Mann Auditorium, Tel Aviv, Israel **27th** Binianei Haooma, Jerusalem, Israel

FAR EAST
November
16th November, National Theatre, Bangkok, Thailand **18th**

Araneta Coliseum Cinema, Manila, Philippines **20th** Academic Hall, Hong Kong **23rd** Kemin Bunka Centre, Ibaragi, Japan **25th** Shi Kokaido, Nagoya, Japan **26th** Kaikan Hall, Kyoto, Japan **27th** Kosei Nenkin Hall, Osaka, Japan **28th** Yubin Chokin Hall, Hiroshima, Japan **30th** Shin-Nittestsu, Taiiku-Kan, Kokura, Japan
December
1st Furitsu Taiiku-Kan, Osaka, Japan **3rd/4th** Budokan, Tokyo, Japan **4th** Budokan, Tokyo, Japan **6th** Kyoshin Kaijo, Sapporo, Japan

CROSSROADS

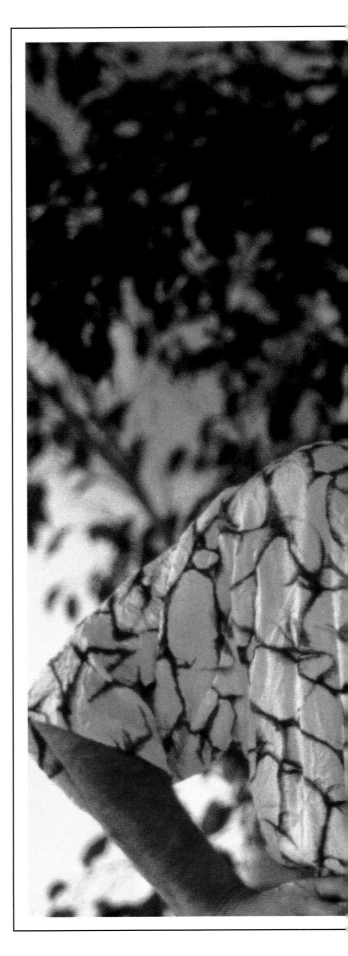

Stagnation set in during the opening years of the Eighties, rooted in Eric's increasing dependence on alcohol. However, once a crash-course cure dragged him back from the abyss, he was almost literally a new man, and the next couple of years involved some spectacular Clapton line-ups in a variety of situations.

There was the British all-star group Gary Brooker and Albert Lee, and an American equivalent with the best of the Stax-style session players.

The three guitar masters, Clapton , Cooder and Lee were matched together, while in complete contrast Eric adopted a backing stance once again, this time in a Roger Waters Pink Floyd project.

August 1983 marked Eric Clapton's 20th Anniversary in the music business. It came just a couple of weeks after he'd been presented with the Silver Clef Award for outstanding achievements in British music, recognising a unique artist who was about to scale new musical heights as the decade progressed.

DIARY

1980
May 2nd-18th
UK tour

1981
January 30th–February 3rd
Irish tour
March 2nd
U.S. tour commences
March 13th
Collapses after concert,
Madison Wisconsin
March 15th
U.S. tour cancelled
September
Secret Policeman's Ball,
London
October 6th–17th
Scandinavian tour
November 16th
West Bromwich Albion
Football Club special
November 27th–December 9th
Japanese tour

1982
January
Enters clinic for alcoholism,
Minneapolis
June 4th–30th
U.S. tour

1983
February 1st–March 3rd
U.S. tour
April 8th–May 24th
U.K./Europe tour
June 24th
Receives Silver Clef Award
June 25th–July 17th
U.S. tour
September 20th/21st
20th Anniversary ARMS
concerts, Albert Hall, London
November 28th–December 9th
U.S. ARMS tour

1984
January 2th–February 6th
European tour
June 16th–July 31st
Roger Waters tour
August 4th
Phill Collins' wedding
November 8th–December 2nd
Australia/Hong Kong
December
Records movie theme for *The Hit*

1985
February 27th–March 15th
U.K./Europe tour
April 9th-July 27th
U.S./Canada tour
May
Records 'Edge of Darkness'
T.V. soundtrack
July 13th
Live Aid, JFK Stadium, Philadelphia
October 5th–12th
Japan/Alaska
October 20th–November 6th
U.K./Europe

THE SHAPE YOU'RE IN

Eric Clapton's music was beginning to sound tired and directionless. The English band was very professional, but seemed better suited to the studio surroundings than the live environment. To give a fresh direction and to breathe a new lease of life into his work, Clapton asked Gary Brooker to join the line-up, relieving Eric of some of the musical responsibility and allowing more space for his guitar work.

Clapton had known Brooker from when the Yardbirds and the Paramounts, Gary's first band, would play the same venues and when Cream and Procol Harum would play on B.B.C. Television's 'Top Of The Pops', and even later during sessions for George Harrison's *All Things Must Pass* album. They didn't meet again until Eric walked into The Parrot Inn in Forest Green, Surrey, where much to his surprise he found Gary behind the bar serving up pints if beer. It was his pub and Clapton became a regular visitor.

Gary Brooker would organize live sessions in his pub and soon Clapton became involved, playing with such people as Mick Fleetwood, Mickey Jupp, Henry Spinetti, Dave Markee, Dave Mattacks, Albert Lee and Mel Collins. The sets would consist of R&B and Americian songs of the 1960s, much to the delight of the 120 or so paying patrons. The Parrot Band, as they were to be called, continued through the years under different names and even now still play when they can, although no longer at the pub which Brooker sold a few years back. Shortly after playing a session for Brooker on a couple of tracks called 'Leave The Candle', and, 'Chasing The Chop', Clapton asked him to join.

In March and April 1980 the new line-up went to Surrey Sounds Studios in Leatherhead for sessions for their new album with Glyn Johns producing. Eric had written some good songs, but somehow in the Surrey environment things just did not sound right. 'Rita Mae' was a sluggish shuffle that needed speeding up to make it work; 'Freedom' was a throwaway song with a half reggae beat that eventually ended up on the soundtrack of a Michael Caine film, *Water*.

Quite a few numbers were written by Gary Brooker such as 'Thunder and Lightning' and 'Home Lovin'', but were not used as RSO did not want them on an Eric Clapton album. Other numbers included 'Evangelina', sung by Albert Lee, that would have been more at home on one of his solo albums, and 'Catch Me If You Can', co-written with Brooker which was a pleasant enough number but didn't really go anywhere. Basically, all the tracks sounded too laid back and the projected album had to be scrapped as RSO felt it was not commercial enough.

Clapton now had to face the fact that in this fickle music business it was hard to sell Sixties survivors, even if they were considered legends by their fans. Punk had changed the music scene completely in England and later in America. The mega-'dinosaur' bands were dying — commercially, and in some cases physically. The Eagles, Led Zeppelin, the Who, for example, were all finding the going tougher. The Rolling Stones seemed to be the only ones to retain their credibility during this period, although even they did not appear live between 1982 and 1989.

Clapton was really doing nothing new with his music and was in need of some inspiration. As soon as the Surrey Sounds sessions finished, he and the band hit the road for a short UK tour starting in Oxford at the New Theatre on 2 May. The only new numbers performed were those that Gary Brooker had written, 'Home Lovin'' and 'Thunder And Lightning'. But Clapton was quite happy to promote and replay his *Just One Night* album for the tour. While the audiences seemed happy enough, his playing lacked the necessary fire.

The final show at the Civic Hall in Guildford held a few surprises, with Clapton and Albert Lee joining the support act Chas and Dave for a version of 'Roll Over Beethoven' and Jeff Beck later joining in during Clapton's set for some interesting guitar work on 'Ramblin' On My Mind'. This was the first time the two had played together in public since Clapton had jammed with the Yardbirds at the Marquee in 1966 after Beck had stepped into his shoes. Although it was an incredible sight to see Eric, Albert and Jeff trading licks, it did not gel as well as might have been hoped for, mainly because their styles were now so far apart. Jeff Beck had long given up his blues-rock beginnings to go down the road of jazz fusion.

With the tour over, Clapton and his band went to

Preceding page: Early Eighties Eric relaxing at home in his Surrey mansion

May 1980, at the penultimate
concert of his British tour, at
London's Hammersmith Odeon

The Daily Mirror *newspaper ran this picture of Eric in February 1981, reporting: 'The man who was a messiah for millions of rock fans is a quiet country squire with a wife and home in Surrey.'*

Compass Point Studios in Nassau to re-record tracks for their next album. Tom Dowd was back in the producer's chair and managed to get more from them all than Glyn Johns had done in Surrey. The location was possibly a major factor, although the best number, 'Say Hello To Billy Jean', a haunting ballad that surely would have been as popular as 'Wonderful Tonight', was inexplicably left off the album. The remainder of the cuts were mainly reworkings of tracks previously done back in Surrey along with a faithful reproduction of Muddy Waters' 'Blow Wind Blow' and a great version of Sleepy John Estes' 'Floating Bridge'. Upon their return, an eight-date tour of Scandinavia was organized, based on the British dates set.

The year started with a short Irish tour. The highlight was a version of Gary's classic hit from his Procol Harum days 'A Whiter Shade of Pale' with Eric playing a solo that sounded as though the song had been written for him. A single date at London's Rainbow Theatre on the 25 February was well attended and acted as a live rehearsal for a huge 57-date tour of America. Yet again, there were few surprises in the set although 'Blow Wind Blow' did feature some inspired playing all round.

Clapton's drinking which had continued on a regular basis from 1974 as his release from heroin, was now taking its toll on him physically, not to mention producing totally unpredictable changes of mood. One minute he would be happy, the next down and completely uncooperative. He had almost reached a point of no return, something which even heroin had not done to him.

Eight dates into his U.S. tour, Clapton collapsed in pain after coming off stage at the Dane County Exposition Center in Madison, Wisconsin. The daily consumption of a bottle of brandy now mixed with painkillers proved to be far too much and he was rushed to hospital for tests on arrival in St Paul.

They revealed that he had ulcers, including one the size of a golf ball, about to burst. The doctors said he could have died at any time. The remainder of the dates were cancelled and his recuperation took around four weeks in St Paul's United Hospital. Shortly after his release, he was involved in a car accident, resulting in several bruised ribs — taking him back to St Paul where they discovered he was also suffering from pleurisy.

The best thing for pleurisy is damp air, so where better than England? Eric flew home and back to his Surrey home with strict orders concerning his diet and definitely no alcohol. He spent some time fishing which he has continued to do whenever possible as an escape from his public life. His new album *Another Ticket* had been released in April, but of course he had no way of promoting it in concert, and as a consequence sales undoubtedly suffered.

FURTHER ON UP THE ROAD

Eric Clapton was not seen in public again until September 1981 when he appeared at the Amnesty International concerts at Drury Lane in London's Covent Garden. Billed as 'The Secret Policeman's Other Ball', the concerts featured some of the best-known British comedians of the time including Billy Connolly, Rowan Atkinson, ex-Monty Python star John Cleese, and John Wells. Between their sketches, various musicians would come on to perform a couple of numbers. Sting, who was effectively musical director, came out to sing unaccompanied versions of 'Roxanne' and 'Message In A Bottle', Phil Collins did 'In The Air Tonight' and 'The Roof Is Leaking' at the piano, Donovan did his Sixties classics 'Universal Soldier' and 'Catch The Wind', a pre-Live Aid Bob Geldof and fellow Boomtown Rat Johnny Fingers performed their No. 1 hit 'I Don't Like Mondays'.

The highlight for Clapton fans was his appearance with Jeff Beck at his side, each performing one of their numbers. Eric on the first night did 'Crossroads' and on the second, 'Further On Up The Road' which featured some great soloing from both, although Beck was the more eloquent on this occasion. In fact, Eric's description of Jeff Beck as a gunslinger is very accurate. On both nights, Beck's number was Stevie Wonder's 'Cause We've Ended As Lovers', with Clapton playing rhythm guitar over Jeff's lead breaks. At the end of the show, the entire cast came out for a rendition of 'I Shall Be Released' led by Sting and featuring a Clapton wah wah solo. The concerts were filmed and recorded, and later released.

In October, he ventured to Scandinavia on his first tour since the aborted American one back in March. The only number performed from the last album was 'Rita Mae', the remainder of the set being the same as on the U.S. dates. The end-of-tour show in Randers, a small town in northern Denmark, featured the usual antics associated with such events. 'Cocaine' was renamed 'Cornflakes' and the encore, 'Further On Up The Road' saw Eric attempting to play the sax!

Back in England, Eric played a special one-off show at the Civic Hall in Wolverhampton on 16 November 1981 for the testimonial of West Bromwich Albion soccer team's John Wile, with the whole team there cheering him on.

Clapton had started to drink heavily again and it came to a crisis point on the Japanese tour that commenced in December, when his body developed an all-over rash brought on by his liver reacting to the intake of alcohol. His manager and friend, Roger Forrester, who had probably aged twenty years in only eight just worrying about him, finally told Eric he would have to be sent to a specialized clinic if there was to be any hope of survival.

Clapton finally agreed to go for help, and in early

January 1982, he and Forrester flew out to Minneapolis. The clinic there was skilled in the treatment of alcoholics and Eric was admitted for an intensive four-week rehabilitation programme, while Roger stayed in a nearby hotel. Part of this programme involved the patient in fending for himself as well as taking part in various mental tests. The main thrust was to keep the alcoholics occupied all the time, not giving them the opportunity of thinking about having a drink, so that by the time the evening rolled around, they would be tired enough to drop off to sleep. After the month, Clapton knew he was better, although not cured. It was going to take immense strength of character to stay dry.

From February until the end of May, Clapton could relax at home, going to the racetrack to watch his horse The Ripleyite and taking in a Ry Cooder concert at London's Hammersmith Odeon, a guitarist he had admired for years. Around this time, he also developed a new passion which became tantamount to a Clapton trademark and remains so to this day — Italian designer clothes. He always had impeccable dress sense right from the Yardbirds onwards and

Clapton during the 1982 American tour, which marked his recovery from alcoholic problems

Albert Lee, along with Clapton one of Britain's rock guitar supremos, seen here backing Eric during the '82 American trek

would often be a trendsetter with people copying his clothes or hairstyle. Together with the new, trendy image and healthier lifestyle, Eric joined Alcoholics Anonymous and devoted much of his time to attending their meetings, particularly during his American tour which started on 4 June 1982 at the Paramount Theater in Cedar Rapids, Iowa.

The set for the tour had not really changed from the last few years, as no new material had been released or indeed recorded. However, so as not to put too much of a strain on him, the shows would normally run for about ninety minutes. On the last date of the tour, in Miami's Sportatorium, Muddy Waters joined Clapton for a version of his 'Blow Wind Blow'. Sadly, this was the last time Eric got to play

with his 'adopted' father who died in April 1983.

After the tour, the whole band flew to Compass Point Studios again, to record a new album. Clapton had locked himself away in a cottage in Wales, without the distractions of his home, to write new songs. When the band rehearsed and tried these out in Nassau, the right feel could not be achieved, resulting in the same lethargic sound that had been with them since 1979. Now sober and focused he realized the time for a change had arrived if he was to progress once again. The majority of the band were fired, with only Albert Lee remaining. The new, assertive Eric Clapton was now not only in control of his life, but also his future.

Tom Dowd was again the album's producer, and

he set about suggesting people to bring in to back Clapton during the sessions. Eventually, they chose Stax house bassist, Donald 'Duck' Dunn who had played with the late and great Otis Redding, Muscle Shoals-based drummer Roger Hawkins who had played with just about everybody of any note, Ry Cooder on slide guitar — simply one of the finest players in the world — and, of course, Albert Lee on guitar and keyboards. Quite a band, which also marked the first step in Clapton's re-emergence as a commercially viable proposition.

The sessions produced some memorable songs including 'The Shape You're In', which was about Patti's drinking problem and featured some good interplay between Eric and Albert. 'Pretty Girl' was another love song about Patti with a beautiful melody, 'Ain't Goin' Down', an up-tempo number which sounds very similar to Jimi Hendrix's arrangement of Dylan's 'All Along The Watchtower', 'Man Overboard', probably the weakest track but redeemed by Cooder's slide playing, and 'Man In Love', done as a blues shuffle celebrating Eric's love for Patti. 'Slow Down Linda' was the most commercial number on the album. The other tracks were faithful cover versions, the best being a copy of Albert King's 'Crosscut Saw' with Eric showing he could still bend those strings.

FROM THE EDGE OF DARKNESS

Clapton's new album *Money And Cigarettes* came out in February 1983 and was promoted with an extensive tour of America, England, Ireland, Europe and then back to America again. The album received good reviews, although the main criticism was that with guitarists of the calibre of Clapton, Cooder and Lee, there should

*Eric takes a bow (**left**) during one of the many standing ovations on the American tour, the climax of which (**above**) was his last ever jam with his hero Muddy Waters, seen here with Clapton and Albert Lee*

■ SET LIST ■

After Midnight • I Shot The Sheriff • Worried Life Blues • Crazy Country Hop • Crosscut Saw • Slow Down Linda • Sweet Little Lisa • Key To The Highway • Tulsa Time • Rock 'n' Roll Heart • Wonderful Tonight • Blues Power • Who's Lovin' You Tonight • Have You Ever Loved A Woman • Ramblin' On My Mind • Let It Rain • Cocaine • Layla • Further On Up On The Road

St. Ouen, Paris, 24 April 1983,
on the European leg of Eric's
'Money and Cigarettes' tour

Prior to the British and
European dates, Clapton
sporting a country-style cut of
the English striped shirt, on
one of the U.S. dates

have been more guitar soloing and general trading of licks. Yet the album was never conceived as a three-pronged guitar battle, rather the new Eric Clapton album.

As such, it offered a new, funkier American sound which had been lacking on previous releases. The touring band featured Albert Lee, 'Duck' Dunn, Roger Hawkins and the reappearance of Chris Stainton. A few dates into the tour, Roger Hawkins had to be replaced by Jamie Oldaker on drums as the road was proving to be hard for him to take. The return of Jamie was a welcome boost to the band. He was already familiar with at least half of the material and quickly learnt the rest. Ry Cooder was the support artist for the American tour, but the prospect of the two guitarists playing together did not materialize except for a show at the Philadelphia Spectrum when Ry joined Eric for 'Crossroads'.

The American tour was promoted by U.S. cigarette manufacturer, Camel, and the American Lung Association not only complained about this, but also the title of the latest album, *Money And Cigarettes* which they felt showed Clapton's neglect of his social responsibilities as a famous person. This controversy

CROSSROADS

aside, the tour carried on smoothly in front of capacity crowds and Eric's playing became more confident. By the time they arrived for the English dates, a lot of the new numbers had been dropped from the set, which meant that England and Europe missed out on a great live rendition of 'Crosscut Saw', which was replaced by 'Lay Down Sally'.

A show at the Civic Hall in Guildford once again proved to be very special. As soon as the band finished the set, an interval took place during which additional amps and a drum kit were brought on. The encores of 'Further On Up The Road' and 'Cocaine' featured the extra talents of Jimmy Page on guitar, playing in public for one of the first times since the demise of Led Zeppelin, and Phil Collins on drums; then came 'Roll Over Beethoven', with Chas and Dave joining, in 'You Win Again', 'Matchbox' and 'Goodnight Irene' which also featured Paul Brady who had been the support artist on the tour.

In June, Clapton also played a short set backed by Chas and Dave's band at the New Victoria Theatre in London for a Save The Children benefit. Clapton has been a regular provider to various charities and prepared to give his services free for worthy causes. A

proud moment for him was on 24 June, when he was presented with the Silver Clef Award for 1983 for outstanding achievement in the world of British music. Princess Michael of Kent did the honours at the eighth Music Therapy Charity lunch in London. Previous winners included the Who, Cliff Richard, Genesis, Elton John, Pink Floyd, Status Quo and the Rolling Stones.

Clapton went back to America in late June to finish his 'Money And Cigarettes' tour. In Chicago, after he had finished his set, he went on to jam with Buddy Guy at the Checker Board Lounge, a tradition that continues whenever the opportunity arises. At the end of the tour, in the beautiful surroundings of the Red Rocks Amphitheater, Denver, support act the Blasters joined him for the encore of 'Further On Up The Road'.

Back home in England, preparations were under way for two special charity concerts to celebrate Clapton's 20th anniversary in the music business and in August, he played on an unusual, but interesting session for Pink Floyd bassist and main songwriter, Roger Waters. The two charity concerts were held at the Royal Albert Hall in London on 20 and 21

The ARMS (Action Research into M.S.) benefit at the Royal Albert Hall, with (left to right) Stevie Winwood, Andy Fairweather-Low, Jimmy Page, Kenny Jones, Clapton, Charlie Watts, Bill Wyman and Jeff Beck

109

'Stones bass player Bill Wyman and Eric during the memorable ARMS gig

body Oughta Make A Change', then on to his trusty Gibson Explorer which had not been seen since the Hammersmith Odeon shows back in December 1974, for 'Cocaine', a blues medley of 'Ramblin' On My Mind/Have You Ever Loved A Woman' and 'Rita Mae', which, incidentally, featured a manic but controlled conga solo by Ray Cooper that was to be a great crowd pleaser well through the late-Eighties into 1990 when Ray was in Clapton's touring band. He played his favourite axe 'Blackie' on the remainder of the set, and he also used a Martin acoustic on the encores of 'Bombers Moon' and 'Goodnight Irene'.

After Eric's set, Andy Fairweather-Low would sang 'Man Smart, Woman Smarter' which was followed by Stevie Winwood's set that included numbers from his recently released solo albums as well as a couple of numbers from his Spencer Davis days such as 'Gimme Some Lovin'', featuring some great playing from Clapton. An interval followed, after which Jeff Beck came on with his band, including Simon Phillips on drums and Fernando Saunders on bass. He effortlessly performed various jazz-influenced instrumentals before surprising everyone by singing his Sixties hit 'Hi Ho Silver Lining' with help from the audience.

Jimmy Page followed, playing nervously, as this was his first large-scale public appearance since the break-up of Led Zeppelin in 1980. The highlight of his set was an emotional instrumental version of the classic 'Stairway To Heaven' after which he was joined by the whole cast who performed 'Tulsa Time', 'Wee

September. The first night was in aid of Eric's friend Ronnie Lane, who was fighting the effects of multiple sclerosis and had helped form Action Research into M.S. — ARMS for short. The second night was for the Prince's Trust, a charity set up to benefit young people in Britain by the Prince of Wales. A lot of major stars offered their services for the shows and it was decided that rather than just jam loosely on various numbers, everyone would do their set with the rest of the artists as a backing band.

The shows were spectacular, bringing together a line up of the rock music élite that would have been almost impossible to present commercially. On drums were Kenny Jones, ex-Faces and ex-Who, and Charlie Watts from the Rolling Stones; on bass was Stone Bill Wyman; on rhythm guitar and vocals Andy Fairweather-Low, ex-Amen Corner heart throb; on percussion the inimitable Ray Cooper; on keyboards were Stevie Winwood (ex-Traffic), Chris Stainton and James Hooker, and on guitar Eric Clapton, Jeff Beck and Jimmy Page.

The opening concert was the better of the two; it lasted just under three hours and was filmed and released on video. Keen Clapton watchers were given an opportunity to see many of his different playing styles as well as his guitars that night. He started on a silver blue Fender Stratocaster for slide on 'Every-

■ SET LIST ■

Royal Albert Hall, London, 20th September, 1983

Everybody Oughta Make A Change • Lay Down Sally • Wonderful Tonight • Ramblin' On My Mind • Have You Ever Loved A Woman • Rita Mae • Cocaine • Man Smart Woman Smarter • Hound Dog • Best That I Can • Road Runner • Slowdown Sundown • Take Me To The River • Gimme Some Lovin' • Tulsa Time • Wee Wee Baby • Layla • Bombers Moon • Goodnight Irene

Wee Baby', and 'Layla'. It was the first time that the three ex-Yardbirds guitarists had performed in public together on the same stage. The final two numbers were sung by Ronnie Lane, greeted by a standing ovation from the crowd who had never witnessed such an event before.

Everyone had such a great time that it was decided to take the whole show to America for a further nine dates in Dallas, San Francisco, Los Angeles and New York. Stevie Winwood was unable to do the American shows because of other commitments and was replaced by Joe Cocker who performed 'Don't Talk To Me', 'Watching The River

Flow', 'Worried Life Blues', 'You Are So Beautiful', 'Seven Days' and 'Feelin' Allright'.

Eric contributed some nice solos during Joe's set. The only other difference between the London shows and those in the States was the appearance of former Free lead singer Paul Rodgers who was now playing in Page's set. (They later formed The Firm together.) Also, during Page's rendition of 'Stairway', both Clapton and Beck would come out to trade guitar solos alongside him on the Led Zeppelin tune, before the whole cast returned to play behind Joe Cocker on his classic 'With A Little Help From My Friends'.

The all-star ARMS band backstage at the Los Angeles Coliseum, including Paul Rodgers, Clapton, James Hooker, Ronnie Lane, Ray Cooper, Andy Fairweather-Low, Joe Cocker, Jimmy Page, Bill Wyman, Chris Stainton, Kenny Jones and Charlie Watts

Joe Cocker, something of a megastar in the U.S.A., fronting the ARMS band during the American concerts

In Dallas, Clapton found time to go to the Tango Club to jam with Lonnie Mack, a guitarist he had long admired,and would have played on Lonnie's first album had other commitments allowed. The ARMS shows at Madison Square Garden had the added bonus of Ronnie Wood playing with Clapton on 'Cocaine', while the encores reunited Wood with his old boss Jeff Beck. Eric most definitely spent his anniversary concerts in good company.

SAME OLD BLUES

*I*n January 1984, Eric Clapton and his band did a short tour, taking in Switzerland, Italy, Yugoslavia, Greece, Egypt and Israel. Now his playing was slowly getting its edge back, and if his new composition 'Same Old Blues'

was anything to go by, we could expect that old fire at any moment. He had once again locked himself away in a Welsh cottage to write the demos for his new album; it was recorded in March and April at Air Studios in Montserrat, West Indies, along with his road band (but not Albert Lee who had decided to go back to his country roots on the Everly Brothers' reunion tour). Guests on the sessions were percussionist Ray Cooper, backing singers Marcy Levy and Shaun Murphy, on synthesizer Peter Robinson and Phil Collins on drums, who was also producing the sessions. Collins and Clapton had been friends since 1978, seeing each other through their bad times like when Phil's marriage broke down; they were regular visitors in each other's homes.

The sessions produced some of Clapton's best playing ever. Two tracks in particular stood out; 'Same Old Blues' and 'Just Like a Prisoner' demonstrated that he was no longer afraid to step out and play guitar. Both were his own compositions.

Other numbers recorded included a wonderful acoustic blues piece called 'Too Bad'; a cover of Eddie Floyd's classic 'Knock On Wood'; a lovely ballad entitled 'Never Make You Cry' which featured Clapton playing a Roland guitar synthesizer for the first time; the Hayes/Porter classic 'You Don't Know Like I Know' with Eric and Phil singing as a duet, and 'One Jump Ahead of the Storm' which had an almost Latin rhythm to it and was definitely one of the better numbers. 'Heaven's Just One Step Away', 'Jailbait', 'She's Waiting', 'It All Depends', and 'Behind The Sun' completed the sessions.

Eric's friend Stephen Bishop was a visitor at Air Studios and recorded a couple of tracks for a forthcoming album with Clapton on guitar and Collins producing.

On his return to England, Clapton rehearsed with Roger Waters for an English, European and American tour to promote the just-released Waters album *The Pros And Cons Of Hitch Hiking*, on which Eric had played back in August 1983. It was a decision that his manager Roger Forrester opposed, asking why should Clapton suddenly play in someone's backing band after having been his own boss since the early Seventies? However, many people did go and see the shows on the strength of Clapton's name and were rewarded with some magnificent playing. He

had at last found the fire which had for so long remained extinguished. It is possible that the continual pain caused by his marital problems, along with the freedom from any leadership responsibilities for the band, gave him that extra edge. Clapton is the first to say that art feeds on personal suffering. This seems to be a strong factor in his career.

The band for the tour comprised Roger Waters on bass and lead vocals, Clapton on lead guitar, Tim Renwick on guitar, Michael Kamen on keyboards,

■ SET LIST ■

Roger Waters U.K. and European tour

Set The Controls For The Heart Of The Sun • Money • If • Welcome To The Machine • Have A Cigar • Wish You Were Here • Pigs On The Wing • In The Flesh? • Nobody Home • Hey You • The Gunners' Dream • 4.30AM • 4.33AM • 4.37AM • 4.39AM • 4.41AM • 4.47AM • 4.50AM • 4.56AM • 4.58AM • 5.01AM • 5.06AM • 5.11AM • Brain Damage

Ron Wood and Jeff Beck reunited during the Madison Square Garden, New York dates of the ARMS tour

guitar was the same that had been churning out so many pleasant but uninspired solos over the previous few years.

After the last date in Europe, Clapton flew back and headed straight to Wembley Stadium in London to play with Bob Dylan alongside Carlos Santana, Mick Taylor, Chrissie Hynde, and Van Morrison. As usual with Dylan, everything was unrehearsed, and during one of the numbers he started the song showing Eric the chords as he went along! Meanwhile, the 'Pros and Cons' tour continued in America for a further ten days. On his return to England, Clapton attended Phil Collins' wedding on 4 August. At the reception, he joined in the jam session alongside Phil, Peter Gabriel and Robert Plant.

In October, Eric assembled the band that he had used earlier in the year for the recording of his new album and spent the month rehearsing for a forthcoming tour of Australasia. The band comprised Clapton on lead guitar and vocals, Duck 'Dunn' on bass, Chris Stainton on keyboards, Peter Robinson on synthesizer, and backing singers Marcy Levy and Shaun Murphy. Marcy had of course been in Eric's band back in the mid-seventies and was at least partially familiar with some of the material. Some new numbers were also previewed, such as 'Knock On Wood', 'You Don't Know Like I Know', 'Tangled In Love', 'She's Waiting' and 'Same Old Blues'. The two girl singers were given a solo spot each, giving Eric a chance to take a breather. They played to capacity crowds and received rave reviews in the press.

Warners in Australia had released 'You Don't Know Like I Know', from the Montserrat sessions, as a single to coincide with the tour. It is the only release this track ever had, so it has become quite a sought-after collectors' item. Warners in America, however, having heard the results of the earlier studio sessions, thought they lacked commercial promise and so offered no potential hit singles. Of course they were wrong. Phil Collins' production had given Clapton a contemporary sound for the first time and the album's original sequence presented to Warners flowed smoothly. 'She's Waiting' was a track begging to be released as a single and had it been, followed by the album in October, enabling it to capture the Christmas market, it would have been an even better seller than when it finally did come out in March 1985 under the title *Behind The Sun*.

Eric during a U.S. date on the 'Pros and Cons of Hitch Hiking' tour

Andy Newmark on drums, Mel Collins on sax, Doreen Chanter and Katie Kissoon on backing vocals and Chris Stainton on keyboards. The stage set-up was quite elaborate, with three huge screens behind the band playing various film sequences and Gerald Scarfe animations relevant to the numbers being performed on the stage at the time.

The show was divided into two parts. The first half consisted of well known Pink Floyd songs with Eric particularly shining on 'Set The Controls For The Heart Of The Sun' and 'Money'. In the second half the band performed the entire *Pros And Cons Of Hitch Hiking* L.P. with Clapton's solo on 'Sexual Revolution' being totally breathtaking. It was hard to think that the man ripping out these notes from his

Warners flew Eric out to Los Angeles to record some additional material which in their eyes could be used as singles. Jerry Williams, a songwriter with a phenomenal ability to produce catchy songs, presented three numbers for him to record. Clapton did not use his own band, but top-line session players such as Toto's Jeff Porcaro and Steve Lukather on drums and rhythm guitar respectively, Fleetwood Mac's Lindsey Buckingham on rhythm guitar, and Nathan East and Greg Phillinganes on bass and synthesizer.

It was Clapton's first recording session with Nathan and Greg who were later to join his band in 1986. He was quite nervous at the prospect of working with these studio pros, but they had admiration and respect for him and made the sessions very memorable. The three numbers recorded were 'Forever Man', 'Something's Happening', and 'See What Love Can Do' and were produced by Warners' Lenny

Waronker and Ted Templeman who also happened to be president and vice president of the company. The tracks were certainly more commercial, but well suited to Eric's style of singing and playing. It is a shame that a complete album could not have been done at these sessions rather than mix them in with the earlier tracks done with his band and a different producer, which only made the project sound disjointed.

He ended the year by recording the theme from the film *The Hit* starring John Hurt as a cool, ruthless hitman. Eric's emotive guitar style suited the mood perfectly and would be the first of many similar projects over the coming years.

The year 1985 marked the beginning of the new high-profile Eric Clapton. He was shocked that Warners rejected the original version of the *Behind The Sun* album and the prospect of being dropped by them was not that unrealistic as they were pruning

Clapton, Andy Newmark, Roger Waters and Tim Renwick during a U.S. date at Nassau Coliseum, Long Island

Above and right: Wembley Arena, London, March 1985; here Clapton received some of the greatest crowd ovations of his career

in 10CC with Graham Gouldman who had written 'For Your Love' back in 1964, the song that gave Eric Clapton the reason to leave the Yardbirds. The video featured Eric and his band who now consisted of a new rhythm guitarist, Tim Renwick, who had accompanied him on the Roger Waters tour. The other significant change was the introduction of a professional lighting system to enhance the music; this was done to great effect during 'Badge' and 'Let It Rain' when hundreds of circular, laser-thin beams of light hit the stage and the audience at varying speeds depending on the tempo of the song. The mood of each song could now be suggested in light while not distracting the listener. The vari-light system was also used by Genesis and Roger Waters.

Eric's six-month separation from Patti resolved itself over the Christmas period and their new-found harmony reflected in his new confidence. Most of 1985 was spent touring the world and at the opening dates at Edinburgh's Playhouse Theatre, Patti could be seen proudly taking photographs of her husband from the box overlooking the stage. In fact she accompanied him for most of the tour.

BLUES BROTHERS

By 1985 Clapton's playing was back at its volatile best. He had never played so consistently well in his entire career. His solos were blistering in the up tempo numbers yet delicate in the more mellow moments during 'Never Make You Cry' and 'Wonderful Tonight'. The usually restrained British audiences were on their feet cheering him on from the first number. Each song was extended with such displays of dexterity that it was difficult to pinpoint a favourite. In London, at the Wembley Arena, actor Dan Aykroyd joined him for the encore of 'Further On Up The Road', introducing Eric and the band in his inimitable style: 'The Bluesbreakers, Blind Faith, Cream, Derek And The Dominos — Ladies and gentlemen, who was the cohesive force behind all these powerhouse bands? He's been called a blues man, he is synonymous with the words electric guitar. Very simply, very finely — Mr Eric Clapton!' Dan said it all.

some of their artists. However, he kept faith with the company's long experience in the hits business.

Jerry Williams' 'Forever Man' was the first single to be released from the new album and another change in direction was the making of a video to promote the single. In the Eighties the success of a single was heavily influenced by the amount of video airplay received on such programmes as the powerful M.T.V. in America and 'Top Of The Pops' in Britain. Because Clapton had never had gimmicks associated with his music, it was decided to do a live performance shoot directed by Kevin Godley and Lol Creme.

Godley and Creme had found fame and fortune

May 1985, and Eric holds an
American audience in awe as
he sings 'Wonderful Tonight'

Clapton conquers America
once again – in New York
(**above**), on the 'Late Night
With Letterman' TV show
(**right**) and at Hartford,
Connecticut (**opposite**)

The tour moved on to Scandinavia and then the United States where he played to sell-out arenas across the country, receiving the best audience response he'd had in years with numerous standing ovations in every performance. At the end of the first half of the tour, he appeared on the influential 'Late Night With Letterman' television programme, playing with the house band. They performed instrumental versions of 'Layla', 'Lay Down Sally', 'White Room', 'Same Old Blues', 'Forever Man', and 'Knock On Wood'. The house band's drummer, Steve Jordan, requested that Clapton do 'White Room' for the show. It was the first time he had performed it since Cream's emotional farewell show at the Royal Albert Hall in London back in 1968 and he enjoyed the experience so much that he included it in his set for the second half of the tour. He introduced it as a number from a hundred years ago. The audiences loved it. Playing Cream numbers was no longer an albatross around Clapton's neck and they were now considered a part of his musical history, not the way his future should be going.

Eric resplendent in a Hawaiian-style shirt during a U.S. date at Richmond, Virginia

At various stages on the American tour ex-members of the E.C. band turned up to jam with their old boss — George Terry in Lakeland, Dick Sims in Providence, and Sergio Pastora in Los Angeles. Other notable jams took place in Chicago with Buddy Guy at the Checker Board Lounge, Carlos Santana played with him on the encore in Concord, Stephen Bishop sang back-up in Costa Mesa and Lionel Richie duetted on 'Knock On Wood' and 'You Don't Know Like I Know' in Seattle. A show from Richmond, Virginia had been recorded for radio broadcast, while

a Hartford, Connecticut concert was filmed and later released on video.

The highlight of the tour and a major boost to his popularity was Clapton's appearance at the J.F.K. Stadium in Philadelphia for the now legendary Live Aid concert in front of 90,000 people and a worldwide television audience of 1.5 billion. The concert was conceived by Bob Geldof to raise money for famine relief in Africa by putting together the biggest ever bill of stars. The show had started in London in front of 72,000 people at Wembley Stadium and followed later on in Philadelphia with images of each show

One of the many performances in Clapton's chequered career to be imortalised on video. This was Hartford, Connecticut, 1 May 1985

*The pan-global Live Aid concerts, with the simple but effective Africa/guitar logo (**below**) captured the imagination of the world, with a roster of star names unequalled before or since*

HARVEY GOLDSMITH, BOB GELDOF AND MAURICE JONES FOR THE BAND AID TRUST PRESENT

AT
**WEMBLEY STADIUM
LONDON**
ADAM ANT
BOOMTOWN RATS
DAVID BOWIE
PHIL COLLINS
ELVIS COSTELLO
DIRE STRAITS
BRYAN FERRY
ELTON JOHN
HOWARD JONES
NIK KERSHAW
ALISON MOYET
QUEEN
SADE
SPANDAU BALLET
STATUS QUO
STYLE COUNCIL
STING
U2
ULTRAVOX
PAUL YOUNG
WHAM!
THE WHO

AT
**J.F.K. STADIUM
PHILADELPHIA**
BRYAN ADAMS
THE CARS
ERIC CLAPTON
DURAN DURAN
BOY GEORGE
HALL AND OATES
MICK JAGGER
BILLY JOEL
WAYLON JENNINGS
JUDAS PRIEST
KRIS KRISTOFFERSON
HUEY LEWIS & THE NEWS
ROBERT PLANT
POWER STATION
PRETENDERS
SANTANA
PAUL SIMON
SIMPLE MINDS
TEARS FOR FEARS
TEMPTATIONS
THOMPSON TWINS
NEIL YOUNG
STEVIE WONDER

**LIVE
AID**

JULY 13th

DOORS OPEN 10 AM, CONCERT STARTS 12 NOON FINISHES 10 PM
Tickets at £25 are on sale NOW from Wembley Stadium Box Office.
And subject to 50p booking fee per ticket and computer fees from
Keith Prowse, Premier London and provincial agencies, Stargreen Agencies.
And BRIGHTON Centre, _____ont, PORTSMOUTH Guildhall, OXFORD Apollo.
And _____ subject to £1 booking fee per ticket from
Keith Prowse Credit Card No 01-741 8999
Or see local press for inclusive coach and concert tickets. Tickets are limited to 6 per person.
DO NOT PAY MORE THAN THE LISTED PRICE FOR YOUR TICKETS.
OUR THANKS TO N.M.E. FOR DONATING THIS PAGE.
NO BOTTLES, NO CANS WILL BE ALLOWED IN THE STADIUM.
ANY DONATIONS WILL BE GRATEFULLY RECEIVED TO 'BAND AID TRUST'
c/o STOY HAYWARD 8 BAKER STREET, LONDON W1M 1DJ.

SOLD OUT

Live Aid represented the highpoint of Clapton's 1985 U.S. appearances, as much for the nature of the event as his own performance, which was nevertheless immaculate

Making his way through security, roadies, press and the inevitable hangers-on, Eric arrives backstage at Live Aid

Just after the historic Philadelphia Live Aid date, on the last week of the 1985 U.S. tour

being relayed on huge video screens in the respective stadiums. It was the world's biggest party.

The huge curtains were pulled back and Clapton launched straight into 'White Room' with a powerful wah-wah solo. This took a lot of people by surprise who maybe had not heard anything by him for a decade and had lost interest in his music. Professional and confident, Eric continued with 'She's Waiting', a powerful number from his latest album, and ended his set with the classic 'Layla'. Phil Collins played drums with his friend after flying over on a specially chartered Concorde from England, having played only a few hours earlier in London.

The energy level was beyond description. Live Aid was an event which all who took part, either as performers, concert goers or television viewers, will remember for the rest of their lives. The final number at J.F.K. Stadium featured Lionel Richie leading most of the day's celebrities, who were jam-packed on stage, in 'We Are The World', with Eric contributing his unique brand of guitar. In fact when the tour ended he did a session for Richie on a track called 'Tonight Will Be Alright' that was released on his *Dancing On The Ceiling* album.

Clapton took a well-deserved holiday in August before preparing for a Japanese tour after which he returned to England via a date in Anchorage, Alaska at the George Sullivan Arena, which he had accepted on hearing that the fishing there was good! A few days after his return, he played a special one-off show at his old stamping ground, the Civic Hall in Guildford where he was joined on the encores by Phil Collins, Carl Perkins and Gary Brooker. He had been rehearsing with Perkins earlier in the day for a television special that was to be filmed the next day. The location of this special concert took place in the Docklands area of London at Limehouse Television Studios in front of a selected audience.

Rock'n'roll guitarist Dave Edmunds was musical director of a band that included Ringo Starr and George Harrison, who themselves were longtime fans of Carl Perkins since their days in the Beatles. Eric came out to play and sing on 'Matchbox', the same number he had played with Carl back in November 1970 on the Johnny Cash television show. The other number featuring Clapton was 'Mean Woman Blues' on which he did an absolutely staggering solo that had Carl and the band nodding in disbelief.

■ SET LIST ■

JFK Stadium, Philadelphia, PA, 13th July 1985,
LIVE AID Broadcast live around the world

White Room • She's Waiting • Layla • We Are The World

Personnel: Eric played guitar behind Lionel Richie and with all the day's performers on stage for the chorus.

Towards the end of the show, the whole band, assembled in a semi-circle on stools, ran through various rockabilly songs. For Carl it was the best way he could have spent the 30th anniversary of his platinum seller 'Blue Suede Shoes'.

Clapton and his band flew out the next day to continue their world tour with dates in Switzerland and Italy. While they were in Italy, the B.B.C. in Britain began its broadcast of a six-part television thriller serial called 'Edge Of Darkness'. He had recorded the soundtrack for the whole series at Pete Townshend's Eel Pie Studios during a break in the U.S. tour back in June. He was shown the images on a studio monitor and played along at various dramatic moments throughout. It was to win him a British Academy of Film and Television Arts award for his soundtrack work on the series. His eerie theme music perfectly matched the story's doomsday scenairo about a nuclear winter.

It had been a gruelling year but his new popularity had turned Clapton into something of a workaholic. On his return to England, he turned up at Dingwalls club in London's Camden Town to play with his old friends Buddy Guy and Junior Wells. At his side was his new girlfriend Lori Del Santo, an Italian model who lived in Milan. This time the split from Patti was for good, finally ending in divorce in 1989.

After the Dingwalls appearance Eric and Lori flew to Milan where Sting invited him up on stage at the Teatro Tenda for a couple of numbers. On his return to England, he played two small charity concerts, the first of which took place in the Dickens pub in Southend, Essex, and the second at the village hall in Dunsfold, Surrey. The band included Gary Brooker on keyboards and vocals, Henry Spinetti on drums, and Mickey Jupp on guitar. Their up-tempo sets were comprised of R&B standards and they called themselves The Pier End Restoration Band.

George Harrison and Eric during the sensational Carl Perkins TV special, which the veteran American rock'n'roller called 'the greatest day of my life'

A rare shot of Eric at leisure, sharing a joke with Mick Jagger at London's Hard Rock Cafe

Still not satisfied, he played with Dire Straits at two of their Christmas shows at the Hammersmith Odeon in London. Special guests had been promised and over the whole period, Paul Young, Hank Marvin and Nils Lofgren played and sang with them at various stages during their set. Eric turned up on the 19 and 22 December to play on 'Two Young Lovers', 'Cocaine', 'Solid Rock' and 'Further On Up The Road', much to the delight of the audience. The pairing of Mark Knopfler and Eric Clapton was to be repeated over the coming years, providing intriguing opportunities to compare the styles of these two contemporary guitar greats.

Incidentally, 'Blackie', Eric's favourite guitar at this time had to be retired around the end of 1985 after 15 years' of faithful service. The neck had worn down and would not have taken the strain of more touring. The only time this guitar gets played now by Eric is in the privacy of his home. Fender made a special Eric Clapton signature model based on his Blackie guitar but with extra features as well. It has Lace Sensor pickups which enables him to sustain, a 22-fret V-shaped neck and three control knobs for volume, tone, and compression. The colours Eric chose for his guitars were Ferrari Red, 7-Up Green and Charcoal Grey.

SINGLES

I Can't Stand It (*Clapton*)
Black Rose (*Seals, Setser*)
U.K. RSO 74/U.S. RSO 1060
Compass Point Studios, Nassau,
Bahamas
July/August 1980
Prod. Tom Dowd
Released February 1981

Another Ticket (*Clapton*)
Rita Mae (*Clapton*)
U.K. RSO 75
Compass Point Studios, Nassau,
Bahamas
July/August 1980
Prod. Tom Dowd
Released April 1981

I've Got A Rock And Roll Heart
(*Seals, Setser, Diamond*)
Man In Love (*Clapton*)
U.K. Duck W9780
Compass Point Studios, Nassau,
Bahamas
September–November 1982
Prod. Tom Dowd
Released January 1983

The Shape You're In (*Clapton*)
Crosscut Saw (*Ford*)
U.K. Duck W9701
Compass Point Studios, Nassau,
Bahamas
September–November 1982
Prod. Tom Dowd
Released April 1983

Slow Down Linda (*Clapton*)
Crazy Country Hop (*Otis*)
U.K. Duck W9651
Compass Point Studios, Nassau,
Bahamas
September–November 1982
Prod. Tom Dowd
Released May 1983

Edge Of Darkness (*Clapton*)
Escape From Northmoor
(*Clapton*)
U.K. BBC RSL 178
Eel Pie Studios, London
May 1st 1985
Prod. Mike Ponczek
Released October 1985

You Don't Know Like I Know
(*Hayes/Porter*)
Knock On Wood (*Floyd/Cropper*)
Air Studios, Montserrat
April 1984
Prod. Phil Collins
Released (Australia only)
November 1984
Forever Man (*William*)
Too Bad (*Clapton*)
U.K. Duck 9069
Lion Share Studios, Los Angeles
December 1984
Air Studios, Montserrat
March–April 1984
*Prods. Ted Templeman/Phil
Collins*
Released March 1985

She's Waiting (*Clapton*)
Jailbait
U.K. Duck 8954
Air Studios, Montserrat
March–April 1984
Prod. Phil Collins
Released June 1985

ALBUMS
JUST ONE NIGHT
Tulsa Time (*Flowers*), **Early In
The Morning** (*arr. Clapton*), **Lay
Down Sally** (*Levy, Clapton*),
Wonderful Tonight (*Clapton*), **If
I Don't Be There By Morning**
(*Dylan*), **Worried Life Blues**
(*Merriweather*), **All Our Past
Times** (*Clapton, Danko*), **After
Midnight** (*Cale*), **Double Trouble**
(*Rush*), **Setting Me Up**
(*Knopfler*), **Blues Power**
(*Clapton, Russell*), **Rambling On
My Mind** (*trad. arr. Clapton*),
Cocaine (*Cale*), **Further On Up
The Road** (*Veasey, Robey*)
U.K. RSO RSDX 2/U.S. RSO RS
2-4202
Live recording, Budokan, Tokyo
December 1979
Prod. Jon Astley
Released May 1980

ANOTHER TICKET
Something Special (*Clapton*),
Black Rose (*Seals, Setser*), **Blow
Wind Blow** (*Morganfield*),

Another Ticket (*Clapton*), **I Can't
Stand It** (*Clapton*), **Hold Me Lord**
(*Clapton*), **Floating Bridge** (*Estes*),
Catch Me If You Can (*Clapton,
Brooker*), **Rita Mae** (*Clapton*),
U.K. RSO 5008/U.S. RSO RX
1-3095
Compass Point Studios, Nassau,
Bahamas
July/August 1980
Prod. Tom Dowd
Released February 1981

MONEY AND CIGARETTES
**Everybody Ought To Make A
Change** (*Estes*), **The Shape
You're In** (*Clapton*), **Ain't Going
Down** (*Clapton*), **I've Got A Rock
And Roll Heart** (*Seals, Setser,
Diamond*), **Man Overboard**
(*Clapton*), **Pretty Girl** (*Clapton*),
Man In Love (*Clapton*), **Crosscut
Saw** (*Ford*), **Slow Down Linda**
(*Clapton*), **Crazy Country Hop**
(*Otis*),
U.K. Duck W 3773
Compass Point Studios, Nassau,
Bahamas
September–November 1982
Prod. Tom Dowd
Released February 1983

BEHIND THE SUN
She's Waiting (*Clapton,
Robinson*), **See What You Can
Do** (*Williams*), **Same Old Blues**
(*Clapton*), **Knock On Wood**
(*Floyd, Cropper*), **Something's
Happening** (*Williams*), **Forever
Man** (*Williams*), **It All Depends**
(*Clapton*), **Tangled In Love**
(*Levy, Feldman*), **Never Make
You Cry** (*Clapton, Collins*), **Just
Like A Prisoner** (*Clapton*),
Behind The Sun (*Calpton*),
U.K. Duck/Warner Bros. 925166-1
Air Studios, Monserrat
Lion Share Studios, Los Angeles
March–April 1984
*Prod. Phil Collins/Ted Templeton
and Lenny Waronker*
Released March 1985

TOURS

1980

May

2nd New Theatre, Oxford **3rd** The Centre, Brighton **4th** Bingley Hall, Stafford **7th** City Hall, Newcastle **8th** The Odeon, Edinburgh **9th** Apollo Theatre, Glasgow **11th** Leisure Centre, Deeside **12th** Coventry Theatre, Coventry **13th** Hippodrome, Bristol **15th–17th** The Odeon, Hammersmith **18th** Civic Hall, Guildford

1981

January

31st Simmonscourt, Dublin

February

1st Leisureland, Galway **2nd** City Hall, Cork **3rd** Youree Youth Centre, Carlow **5th** Rainbow Theatre, London

March

2nd Memorial Coliseum, Portland, Oregon **3rd** The Coliseum, Spokane, Washington **5th–7th** Paramount Theater, Seattle, Washington **9th** Yellowstone Metra, Billings, Montana **10th** The Four Seasons Arena, Great Falls, Montana **13th** Dane County, Expo. Center, Madison, Wisconsin **14th** Arena Auditorium, Duluth, Minnesota **15th** Civic Center Arena, St. Paul, Minnesota

October

6th Depart for Helsinki **7th** Icehall, Helsinki, Finland **9th** Isstadion, Stockholm, Sweden **10th** Scandinavium, Gothenburg, Sweden **12th** Drammenshallen, Oslo, Norway **13th** Olympen, Lund, Sweden **15th** Forum, Copenhagen, Denmark **16th** Vejlby-Risskovhallen, Aarhus, Denmark **17th** Randershallen, Randers, Denmark

November

16th Wolverhampton, Civic Hall **30th** Dichi Kosei Nenkin Hall, Nagoya

December

1st Festival Hall, Osaka **3rd** Sun Palace, Fukuoka **4th** Kaikan Dai - Ichi Hall, Kyoto **7th** Budokan Theatre, Tokyo **8th** Bunka Taiiku-Kan, Yokohama **9th** Budokan Theatre, Tokyo

1982

June

5th Paramount Theater, Cedar Rapids, Iowa **6th** Civic Audiotrium, Omaha, Nebraska **7th** Met. Center, Minneaspolis, Minnesota **10th–11th** Pine Knob, Birmingham, Michigan **12th** Memorial Auditorium, Buffalo, New York **13th** Blossom Music Theater, Cuyahoga Falls **17th** Cumberland Civic Center,

Portland, Maine **18th** Broome County Coliseum, Binghamton, N.Y. **19th** Performing Arts Center, Saratoga, New York **22nd** Hampton Roads Coliseum, Hampton, Virginia **23rd** The Coliseum, Charlotte, North Carolina **24th** Viking Hall, Bristol, Tennessee **27th** The Civic Center, Augusta, Georgia **28th** The Coliseum, Jacksonville, Florida **29th** The Civic Center, Lakeland, Florida **30th** The Sportatorium, Hollywood, Florida

1983

February

1st/2nd The Paramount Theater, Seattle **3rd** The Civic Center, Portland **6th** The Convention Center Auditorium, Sacramento **7th** The Cow Palace, San Francisco **8th** The Universal Ampitheatre, Los Angeles **9th** The Long Beach Arena, Long Beach **11th** Veterans Memorial Coliseum, Phoenix **13th** Special Events Center, Austin **14th** The Summit, Houston **15th** Reunion Arena, Dallas **17th** The Mid-South Coliseum, Memphis **18th** Keil Auditorium, St. Louis **19th** Hara Arena, Dayton **21st** The Spectrum, Philadelphia **22nd** Byrne Arena, East Rutherford **25th** The Omni, Atlanta **26th** The Gardens, Louisville **28th** The Capitol Center, Washington

March

1st The Centrum, Worcester **2nd** The Hershey Park Arena, Hershey **3rd** The Civic Arena, Pittsburgh

April

8th/9th The Playhouse, Edinburgh **11th** City Hall, Newcastle **12th** Empire, Liverpool **14th–16th** The Stadium, Dublin **20th** Stadthalle, Bremen **21st** Grugahalle, Essen **23rd** Ahoy, Rotterdam **24th** Chateau de Pontin, Paris **26th** Sporthalle, Cologne **27th** Festhalle, Frankfurt **29th** Rhein Necker Halle, Eppelheim **30th** St. Jakobshalle, Basle

May

2nd Palasport, Rome **3rd**

Palasport, Genoa **5th** Sport Palladium, Toulouse **7th** Sportspalace, Barcelona **8th** Velodromo, San Sebastian **13th** Cornwall Coliseum, St. Austell **14th** Poole Arts Center, Poole **16th–19th** Hammersmith Odeon **21st** Manchester Apollo, Manchester **22nd** De Montfort Hall, Leicester **24th** Civic Hall, Guildford

June
25th Kingswood Music Theater, Toronto
27th–29th Pine Knob, Detroit

July
1st Performing Arts Center, Saratoga Springs **2nd/3rd** Jones Beach, Long Island, New York **5th** Merriweather Post Pavilion, Columbia **7th** Blossom Music Theater, Cleveland **9th** Civic Center, St. Paul **10th** Milwaukee Festival, Milwaukee **11th** Poplar Creek, Chicago **13th** Kings Island Timberwolf Theatre, Cinn. **14th** Wings Stadium, Kalamazoo **16th/17th** Red Rocks Amphitheatre, Denver

1984
January
20th/21st Hallenstadion, Zurich, Switzerland
23rd/24th Teatro Tenda, Milan, Italy
26th Beogradski-Sajam Hala, Belgrade, Yugo.
28th/29th Sporting of Athens, Athens, Greece
February
2nd American University, Cairo, Egypt
5th/6th B'Nai Haooma, Jerusalem, Israel
ROGER WATERS TOUR
June
16th/17th Ice Stadium, Stockholm
19th Ahoy Theatre, Rotterdam
21st/22nd Earls Court, London
26th/27th N.E.C., Birmingham
July
3rd Hallenstadium, Zurich **6th** Palais De Sport, Paris **17th/18th** Civic Center, Hartford, Connecticut **20th/22nd** Meadowlands Arena, New Jersey **24th** Spectrum, Philadelphia **26th** Stadium, Chicago **28th/29th** Maple Leaf Gardens, Toronto **31st** Forum, Montreal

November
13th/14th Horden Pavilion, Sydney **17th** Festival Hall, Brisbane **20th/21st** Hordern Pavilion, Sydney **23rd–25th** Sports & Entertainments Centre, Melbourne **28th** Entertainment Centre, Perth
December
2nd The Coliseum, Hong Kong

1985
February
27th/28th The Playhouse, Edinburgh, Scotland
March
N.E.C., Birmingham, England **4th/5th** The Arena, Wembley, London **9th** The Icehall, Helsinki, Finland **12th** Valbyhallen, Copenhagen, Denmark **15th** Isstadion, Stockholm, Sweden

U.S.A. TOUR
April
9th Convention Center, Dallas, Texas **10th** The Summit, Houston, Texas **11th** South Park Meadows, Austin, Texas **13th** Civic Center, Pensacola, Florida **15th** Civic Center, Lakeland, Florida **16th** James Knight Center, Miami, Florida **18th** Duke University, Durham, North Carolina **19th** Civic Center, Savannah, Georgia **20th** The Omni, Atlanta, Georgia **22nd** Coliseum, Richmond, Virginia **23rd** Civic Center, Baltimore, Maryland **25th** Bryne Arena, Meadowlands, New Jersey **26th** Coliseum, Nassau, Long Island **28th** Civic Center, Providence, Rhode Island **29th** The Spectrum, Philadelphia, Pennsylvania
May
1st Civic Center, Hartford, Connecticut
2nd Cumberland County Civic Center, Portland
3rd The Forum, Montreal, Quebec
June
21st Kingswood Ampitheatre, Toronto, Ontario **22nd** Cleveland Blossom Music Theater Ohio **23rd** Rochester Music Center, New York State **25th** Performing Arts Center, Saratoga, NYS **26th** The Centrum, Worcester,

Massachusetts **27th** Merriweather Post Pavilion, Columbia, Maryland **28th** Garden State Arts Centre, Holmdel, NJ **30th** The Summer Festival, Milwaukee, Wisconsin
July
1st The Gardens, Louisville, Kentucky **2nd/3rd** Pineknob, Detroit, Michigan **5th** Poplar Creek, Chicago, Illinois **6th** Music Center Ampitheatre, Indianapolis, Indiana **7th** River Bend Music Center, Cincinnati, Ohio **9th** Amphitheatre, Kansas City, Kansas **11th** Red Rocks, Denver, Colorado **13th** J.F.K. Stadium, Philadelphia, Pennyslvania **14th** Red Rocks, Denver, Colorado **17th/19th** Universal Ampitheatre, Los Angeles California **21st** Compton Terrace, Phoenix, Arizona **22nd** Pacific Ampitheatre, Costa Mesa, California **23rd/24th** Concord Pavilion, San Francisco, California **26th** Coliseum, Seattle, Washington
October
5th/6th Olympic Pool, Yoyogi, Tokyo, Japan **7th** Koseinenkin, Osaka, Japan **9th** Shimin Kaikan, Nagoya, Japan **10th** Festival Hall, Osaka, Japan **11th** Sun Palace, Fukuoka, Japan **14th** George Sullivan Arena, Anchorage, Alaska **20th** Civic Hall, Guildford, Surrey, England **23rd** Halle Des Fetes, Lausanne, Switzerland **24th** Hallenstadion, Zurich, Switzerland **27th/28th** Theatre Tenda, Milan, Italy **29th** Palasport, Turin, Italy **31st** Palasport, Caserta, Naples, Italy
November
1st Palaeur, Rome, Italy
2nd Palasport, Genova, Italy
4th Theatre Tenda, Bologna, Italy
5th Palasport, Florence, Italy
6th Palasport, Padova, Italy

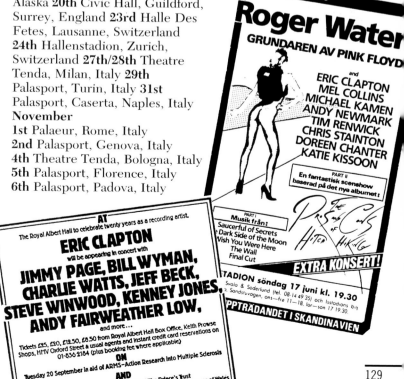

CLAPTON TODAY

*T*he late Eighties and early Nineties have represented the peak of Eric Clapton's considerable achievements so far.

As well as gathering round him some of the best musicians in contemporary rock, he has branched out into film music, television work, not to mention his now-annual seasons at London's Royal Albert Hall in which he features performances in rock, blues and orchestral formats.

His status has been recognised both in awards of various kinds, and his invited presence to prestigious events like the Princes Trust concerts, the Nelson Mandela 70th Birthday concert, and even Chuck Berry's 60th Birthday!

As instrumental virtuoso, vocal stylist and highly creative band musician, still with his roots in the blues, the Clapton story goes on and on. . . . .

DIARY

1986
February 23rd
Ian Stewart memorial, 100
Club London
June 20th
Princes Trust concert,
Wembley, London
July
European tour
October 18th
Chuck Berry 60th Birthday
concert

1987
January
6 nights, Albert Hall, London
January 26th–30th
Italy
February 9th
BPI Awards, London
April
U.S. tour
June 5th/6th
Princes Trust, Wembley,
London
July
BBC Radio 1 biography series
October
Australia/Japan

1988
January
Albert Hall dates, London
April
Movie soundtrack, *Homeboy*
June 6th
Princes Trust, Albert Hall,
London
June 8th/9th
Dire Straits concerts
June 11th
Nelson Mandela 70th Birthday
concert
September 1st–October 8th
U.S. tour
October 26–November 6th
Japan

1989
January–February
Royal Albert Hall, London
March 7th
Soundtrack, *License To Kill*
July 6th–30th
Europe/Africa
December
Title music, 'Communion'

1990
January 18th–February 10th
Albert Hall, London
Feburary 14th–March 5th
Europe
March 28th–August 16th
U.S. tour
September
South America
November–December
Australia, Asia and Far East

1991
January/February
24 nights, Albert Hall, London

PRINCES AND KINGS

Prince's Trust Concert
Wembley Stadium, London
June 20th 1986

*T*he year started sadly for Eric Clapton with the death of his friend and occasional band mate, Ian Stewart, from a heart attack. Ian was always known as 'the sixth Stone', playing on all the group's records and even accompanying them from off stage on their early tours. His piano style was as well known as it was loved, as indeed was the man. As a tribute, the Rolling Stones organized a jam session to end all jam sessions at the 100 Club in London's Oxford Street on 23 February. Pete Townshend and Eric Clapton joined them for 'Down The Road A Piece' and 'Hoochie Coochie Man', after which Jeff Beck joined in for Howlin' Wolf's 'Little Red Rooster'. Eric, playing a Sunburst Fender Stratocaster, delivered precise solos throughout the set and was joined by his old Cream colleague Jack Bruce for a

rousing version of Chuck Berry's 'Little Queenie'. 'Stew' would have loved it.

A couple of days later Clapton appeared live on television to present his old friends, the Rolling Stones, with a Lifetime Achievement award at the Roof Gardens in Kensington. Both Clapton and the Stones were survivors of their era and would continue on to even greater heights.

In April Eric went to record his next album at Sunset Sound in Los Angeles. His touring band had gone as far as they could and it was time for another change. Clapton wanted to appeal to more than just the steady fans and reach an even wider audience. He found in Nathan East and Greg Phillinganes two exceptionally talented and creative musicians that would keep him on his toes. He had met the two originally during the additional *Behind The Sun* sessions in Los Angeles and had been greatly impressed by them. Phil Collins was brought in to complete the quartet as drummer and producer.

The sessions resulted in a new Clapton sound,

Preceding page: *Knebworth, 1990, one of the many high points of Clapton's recent career.*

Right: *Likewise the Prince's Trust Concert of 1986 when Eric duetted with the dynamic Tina Turner*

largely due to his songwriting collaboration with Greg on most numbers as well as his choice of other people's material to record. One of the most lyrically powerful songs was 'Holy Mother', comparable to his 'Presence Of The Lord' song, which had equally religious connotations. Another number recorded, 'Lady Of Verona', about his Italian girlfriend Lori Del Santo, sounded like a raunchy Chuck Berry-style rocker. Although it remains unreleased, it reveals much about the relationship he had with Lori and presented a real contrast to the romantic songs he wrote for Patti.

Tina Turner guested on two numbers, 'Tearing Us Apart' and 'Hold On'. A horn section was used on most of the sessions, for the first time since the *Eric Clapton* album in January 1970.

Once the recording was finished, he came back to England to appear at the Tenth Birthday Party of the Prince's Trust held at Wembley Arena on the 20 June. Big Country, Suzanne Vega, and Level 42 opened the show and after the interval, the audience were treated to an amazing array of superstars coming on one after the other. The backing band consisted of Mark Knopfler on guitar, Phil Collins on drums, John Illsley on bass, Midge Ure on guitar, Howard Jones on keyboards, Ray Cooper on percussion and of course Eric Clapton on lead guitar.

Tina Turner was first on singing 'Better Be Good To Me', and stayed on to duet with Clapton on his new number, 'Tearing Us Apart', which had her hamming it up with Eric at the microphone. It was the first time he had played it live and it was to become a stage favourite over the coming years. Next, he introduced the musical director Midge Ure, who sang his latest single, 'Call Of The Wild'. Sting joined Mark Knopfler for a version of the Dire Straits classic 'Money For Nothing' with a solid backing driving it along before quietening things down for Paul Young singing 'Everytime You Go Away'. Joan Armatrading came next for 'Reach Out', followed by Howard Jones singing his Phil Collins-produced single, 'No One Is to Blame'.

Rod Stewart followed to sing his biggest hit 'Sailing' which featured a beautifully emotive solo by Clapton. The crowd, who had been on their feet from the start singing along to the numbers they knew so well, could not believe their luck at being at such an event. Elton John sang his 'I'm Still Standing' next,

after which Paul Young came out again to sing 'Every Time You Go Away' once more, this time as a duet with Wham!'s George Michael.

Then the first real surprise came when Rick Parfitt, Francis Rossi and Bryan Adams joined the backing band for the appearance of Paul McCartney who stormed into 'I Saw Her Standing There', quickly followed by another rocker, 'Long Tall Sally'. Surely that must have been it? But no — on came David Bowie and Mick Jagger to sing the number they had previewed on video at the Live Aid concert, 'Dancing In The Street'. Though totally unrehearsed and their appearance unscheduled, it was an unexpected and fantastic opportunity to see them live.

Paul McCartney then concluded with the Beatles' classic 'Get Back' and with this the magical evening was over. A line-up of both historic and contemporary rock stars had converged to perform in an arena that any one of them could have sold out singlehandedly many times over. The event was filmed and recorded for later release.

Clapton'a new album was originally to be called *One More Car, One More Rider* and to promote it, the band that recorded it rehearsed for a festival tour

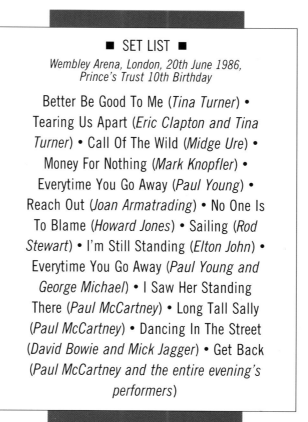

■ SET LIST ■

*Wembley Arena, London, 20th June 1986,
Prince's Trust 10th Birthday*

Better Be Good To Me (*Tina Turner*) •
Tearing Us Apart (*Eric Clapton and Tina Turner*) • Call Of The Wild (*Midge Ure*) •
Money For Nothing (*Mark Knopfler*) •
Everytime You Go Away (*Paul Young*) •
Reach Out (*Joan Armatrading*) • No One Is To Blame (*Howard Jones*) • Sailing (*Rod Stewart*) • I'm Still Standing (*Elton John*) •
Everytime You Go Away (*Paul Young and George Michael*) • I Saw Her Standing There (*Paul McCartney*) • Long Tall Sally (*Paul McCartney*) • Dancing In The Street (*David Bowie and Mick Jagger*) • Get Back (*Paul McCartney and the entire evening's performers*)

Abroad in Europe: relaxing with Phil Collins (**right**) during the 1986 Continental tour, and (**far right**) during the soundcheck at the Antibes Jazz Festival in the South of France

of Scandinavia and Europe. The five shows took place in Oslo in Norway, Copenhagen in Denmark, Montreux in Switzerland and Juan Les Pins in France. The date in Montreux at the famous Casino was probably one of the best shows Eric had ever done. During 'The Same Old Blues', Greg and Nathan came into their own with some exceptional improvising and Phil Collins providing solid drumming.

Clapton's guitar sound had changed and now had a harder edge to it. On the eve of his performance at the Montreux Jazz Festival, he jammed with one of his heros, Otis Rush, and even got to sing on 'Double Trouble'. The entire Otis Rush performance was broadcast live on Swiss radio and a portion later shown on Swiss television, including two numbers with Clapton.

He brought the band back to England for two amazing shows at the N.E.C in Birmingham on 14 and 15 of July which were recorded for a possible live album. Also, the second concert was filmed and later released as a one-hour video.

The tour had given them the opportunity to preview the newly recorded material to judge audience response. Most people liked the new sound and choice of material which now included the Cream nugget 'Sunshine Of Your Love'. In fact, four Cream numbers were now in the set, the others being

'Crossroads', 'White Room', and 'Badge'. Collins performed his song 'In The Air Tonight', one of the many highlights of the lengthy show.

Clapton was now having to play more without the help of a rhythm guitarist, which gave him even more responsibility. In July, he was asked to contribute some music for use in a new Paul Newman and Tom Cruise movie called *Color Of Money*, a sequel to the film Newman had starred in many years before, *The Hustler*. Clapton recorded two songs, 'The Gift (It's In The Way That You Use It)' with Gary Brooker on keyboards and backing vocals, Henry Spinetti on drums, Laurence Cottle on bass, and Richard Cottle on synthesizer; and 'It's My Life Baby', recorded with the Big Town Playboys, an English band who play authentic R&B. Unfortunately, when the film came out, the songs were buried in the mix and could hardly be heard.

'It's In The Way That You Use It' was released as a single in America with a promotional video showing clips from the movie intercut with Eric playing his guitar. The second number recorded for the film remains unreleased, but was a great blues shuffle that suited the guitarist's style perfectly.

In August, he went to see Prince in concert at Wembley Arena. Clapton greatly admired Prince as a musician, so when he was asked to play the same evening at the after-show party, he jumped at the opportunity. He was amazed at Prince's dexterity at the drums, keyboards and guitar, and played on the Al Green song 'Can't Get Next To You'. Prince rarely plays his own compositions at these parties, preferring to perform numbers by people who have influenced him, such as 'Red House' by Jimi Hendrix, and 'Sex Machine' by James Brown.

Early that month, Clapton played a charity cricket match that also saw Mick Jagger on the pitch, at Finchley Cricket Club in north London. He exchanged his bat for a guitar in the evening when he jammed with Stan Webb's Chicken Shack in the marquee that had been set up in the grounds of the club. Stan had a long history of blues playing, making some fine albums over the years despite real success eluding him.

The next day, Eric, Phil, Greg and Nathan went to Ronnie Scott's club in London's Soho to film a video for their British single, 'Tearing Us Apart'.

With an invitation-only audience, it was assumed that it would be a live shoot with full stage shots. In fact, the finished product only showed close-ups of various members' hands and lips as well as the fishnet stockings belonging to a model hired to simulate Tina Turner who is featured on the track. The video was never released, although Warners did put out a few promotional copies. While the cameramen were reloading, Eric and friends treated the audience to various instrumentals, including a spirited version of Prince's '1999', while Greg and Nathan also did their comedy routine of wisecracking one-liners.

At the end of August, Clapton went to the Townhouse Studios in London to record tracks for Bob Dylan's forthcoming film, *Hearts Of Fire*. Also participating at the session were Ronnie Wood on bass and Henry Spinetti on drums. Over a two-day period, they recorded seven takes of 'Had A Dream About You', which sounded remarkably like 'Clean Cut Kid' from Bob's *Empire Burlesque* album; three

Phil Collins towers over Eric, Greg and Nathan during the spectacular night at the Birmingham National Exhibition Centre in England

takes of 'The Usual'; one take of an untitled track simply labelled 'Song With No Name'; three takes of 'Five And Dimer' and one take of 'To Fall In Love'.

Eric rarely turns down the opportunity to 'sit in' with artists he admires, and the Lionel Richie date at Madison Square Garden was no exception

■ **SET LIST** ■
Chuck Berry's 60th Birthday
Fox Theatre, St. Louis, Missouri,
16th October 1986

Wee Wee Hours • Rock And Roll Music •
Hail! Hail! Rock 'N' Roll

The sessions were typical of Dylan, running through numbers as quickly as possible with minimal rehearsal. Clapton's contribution was largely rhythm work rather than lead. Additional horns and keyboards were added at a later stage for the soundtrack album.

Another session he contributed to around this time was for Bob Geldof's first solo album, which featured some of Eric's best studio playing to date. Bob Geldof, who had given Eric carte blanche, was awestruck by his abilities and even remarked, quite correctly, that his playing had not been so intense since the Dominos period. Bob's eponymous album, *Deep In The Heart Of Nowhere*, came out in November with Clapton appearing on four tracks. The first single to be released from it was 'Love Like A Rocket'. Eric not only appeared in the video, but also turned up with Bob live on a British kids' television programme, called 'Saturday Superstore' to perform the single.

In October, Clapton was invited to perform in two special concerts for Chuck Berry's 60th Birthday Celebration which took place at the Fox Theatre in St Louis. There have been many stories and rumours concerning Chuck — some true, some false — but it is a fact that the chip on his shoulder is equal to his talent. To say he is erratic and hard to work with, is an understatement.

Clapton had searched out an extremely rare Gibson ES-350T which is the guitar Berry used on all his early recordings. It is also featured on many of his early album covers and publicity photographs. The 'T' stands for 'Thin' and the guitar had a 2¼-inch-deep body, humbucking pickups, a short-scale maple neck with a laminated maple top, a rosewood fingerboard, a looped style tailpiece and gold-plated hardware. In short, a beautiful instrument — and when Eric showed Chuck his new acquisition like a proud kid, Chuck showed no interest at all!

The musical director was Berry's greatest admirer, Keith Richards, who had the unenviable task of putting the whole thing together. Keith must have aged ten years trying to get him to rehearse and when things finally looked and sounded right a few days before the shows, he started to relax. Unfortunately, on the day, Berry forgot about the rehearsals and played it his way!

Still, with such a line-up it could not fail to be good. Included in the band were Chuck's original piano player, Johnnie Johnson, Keith Richards on guitar, Joey Spampinato on bass, Steve Jordan on drums, Chuck Leavell on keyboards, Bobby Keys on saxophone and Chuck's daughter, Ingrid, on additional vocals. Special guests came out to perform some of Chuck's greatest hits from his extensive back catalogue. These included 'Brown Eyed Handsome Man' sung by Robert Cray, 'Rock And Roll Music' sung by the ever powerful Etta James and the bluesy 'Wee Wee Hours' played and sung by Eric Clapton featuring a vicious solo on his 350T.

After the shows, Eric stayed in New York for promotional work including various interviews, one of which was on 'Nightlife' where he played with the house band that included his old friend Billy Preston on keyboards. The numbers they played were 'Miss You', 'It's In The Way That You Use It' and 'I Shot The Sheriff'. While in New York he also took the opportunity to see his friend Lionel Richie at Madison Square Garden. He was invited up for a version of 'Tonight Will Be Alright', the song Eric had contributed to on Richie's latest album.

ONE MORE CAR

With 'blood brother' Keith Richards during the first of the Ritz dates in New York City

On his return to England, Clapton went to see Robert Cray at London's Mean Fiddler pub and inevitably ended up playing with him on 'Smoking Gun', 'Playing In The Dirt', 'The Last Time', 'Bad Influence' and 'Phone Booth'. The last number was included as a free flexi-disc with an issue of the American *Guitar Player* magazine. It was the third time that Clapton had played with Cray, the first was at the Montreux Jazz Festival back in July on Eric's encore, as was the second time at the N.E.C. in Birmingham.

Eric's new album, *August*, inappropriately came out in November to critical acclaim and went gold within weeks. He had at long last achieved mass acceptance picking up a whole new generation of fans who had not even been born when Cream expired. The album's title was changed from *One More Car, One More Driver* to *August* as a celebration of the birth of his son Conor that month to Lori Del Santo. The record company added the number he'd re-

corded for the *Color of Money* soundtrack, 'It's In The Way That You Use It' on the new album. Unfortunately it was out of place, having been recorded at a different time with a different band to the rest of the tracks. Consequently, the feel was substantially different and should not have replaced the original choice of 'Wanna Make Love To You' which Clapton had previewed in concert as being from the new album. The track eventually surfaced on Polygram's excellent 'Crossroads' boxed set.

To coincide with the release of *August* in the U.S.A., Clapton went back to his roots by playing a few selected club dates at the Metro in Boston and the Ritz in New York. He had not played to such a small crowd in a long time. It was also the first appearance of Steve Ferrone on drums who had played with the Average White Band, Duran Duran and on countless sessions. The four-piece was completed by Nathan East and Greg Phillinganes. They played two shows at each venue, all four shows were magical and people lucky enough to get hold of the hottest tickets in town were rewarded with some extraordinary playing. In New York, even the bitter cold and snow could not keep people away, including some who had queued all afternoon hoping for ticket returns. At the first of the Ritz shows, Clapton introduced Keith Richards as his 'blood brother', who joined in for a couple of numbers. Keith and his trusty Fender Telecaster played a great solo in 'Cocaine' but got a little lost in the complicated chord changes on 'Layla'.

On his return to England, Clapton layed down some guitar parts for the forthcoming Mel Gibson film *Lethal Weapon*, before ending the year by playing a charity show with Gary Brooker and friends at the village hall in Dunsfold, Surrey.

Early in 1987 Eric Clapton played two shows at the Apollo in Manchester, followed by six nights at London's Royal Albert Hall. The big surprise was the appearance of Mark Knopfler in the band. Mark had asked Eric if he could come by for a play to which Eric thought he meant just a jam on the encore. In fact, to his surprise and great pleasure Mark meant the whole performance and the whole tour, as part of the band!

Clapton had, of course, guested with Dire Straits back in 1985 and was familiar with Knopfler's technique and style. It was amazing to see such guitar giants at work together and the audiences were also suprised and overjoyed. A few more of Eric's friends were to drop by. Sting and Stevie Winwood joined in the encores on the third night at the Albert Hall for 'Money For Nothing' and 'Sunshine Of Your Love'. The last three nights at the Albert Hall were recorded on the Rolling Stones Mobile Studio for a planned double live album which sadly to date remains unreleased. The reason for this was that soon two collections of his greatest hits would be put out, *The Cream Of Eric Clapton* and the retrospective boxed set *Crossroads*; a third would simply have glutted the market. Although it had not reached the artwork stage, the track selection had been made by Eric's sound engineer, Mike Ponczek, who also produced the live material. It would have been a fair representation of the E.C. shows from this period and compiled

Clapton's Albert Hall concert dates early in the New Year have now become an annual event, and something of an institution in the rock music calendar

George Harrison greets Eric
backstage during the 1987
Royal Albert Hall season

from concerts in Montreux, Birmingham, London and, from later in 1987 Providence and New York.

A European tour followed to massive praise in the music press with headlines such as 'God Is Back At Last!' The last time he had played Europe in 1978, the reviews had not been so favourable and had basically written him off as another Sixties casualty. Clapton proved them wrong and returned stronger than ever.

After the tour finished, he returned home and attended the British Phonographic Institute Awards at the Royal Albert Hall on 9 February where he was presented with an award for his services to music. Over the years he has received many accolades and is proud to be recognized for doing what he enjoys best — playing the guitar.

He spent some time in February recording with Jack Bruce for a solo album his ex-Cream colleague was preparing. They also played a two-hour-plus impromptu concert on Clapton's patio which was filmed for inclusion on a 'South Bank Show' television special that was being made on Eric's life. February also found Eric riding high in the singles chart with 'Behind The Mask', leading his appearance on 'Top Of The Pops' for the first time since Cream in 1967. He looked just as uncomfortable now as he had back then, miming to the backing track in front of a group of dancing kids. However, it gained him a further legion of fans who were in many cases unaware of his past and only interested in his future.

In March, preparations were underway for a 13-date tour of America with Phil Collins back in the drummer's seat. Before undertaking the tour Clapton played a small charity concert at the Cranleigh Golf Club in Surrey with local friends. The set included his hit single 'Behind The Mask' and more unusual titles not normally performed by him such as 'Route 66', Peter Green's 'Black Magic Woman', 'Walkin' The Dog', 'The Bear' and 'Walkin' On Sunset'. The small oak beamed room with an open fireplace was a million miles away from the opening date of the U.S. tour at the massive Oakland Stadium in California. The only similarity was in Eric's playing.

The support group for the tour was Robert Cray and his band, resulting in several jams on Clapton's encore of 'Further On Up The Road'. He and Collins participated in a film for a B.B. King television special at the Ebony Showcase Theater in Los Angeles on 15 April. Also playing at the show were Stevie Ray Vaughn, Albert King, Paul Butterfield, Dr. John and Etta James. The highlight for Clapton fans was the version of 'The Thrill Is Gone' with some great interplay between King and Clapton.

A few days later, after his show in Chicago, Clapton together with Robert Cray and Phil Collins went to the Limelight club for a jam with Buddy Guy which included a rather shaky version of Cream's 'Strange Brew'. The last two shows of this mini tour at the Civic Center in Providence and Madison Square Garden in New York were recorded for the aborted live album project.

On his return to Britain, he played at a special

The final night of the U.S. tour, 27 April 1987, which climaxed at New York's Madison Square Garden. Star support act was Robert Cray **(left)**, who joined Eric on his penultimate number 'Further On Down the Road'
Below: An encore bow with Phil Collins

Lionel Richie Prince's Trust concert at London's Wembley Arena on 'Tonight Will Be Alright' and the old Commodores number 'Brickhouse'. To confirm Clapton's greatly increased popularity, the audience who a few years back may not have been that familiar with his name were now ecstatic at his presence.

On 5 and 6 June the Prince's Trust concerts took place again at London's Wembley Arena. They were similar in style to the previous year's anniversary show with Clapton again playing the lead guitar in the supergroup backing band that included Phil Collins, Level 42's Mark King on bass, musical director Midge Ure on guitar, Ray Cooper on percussion and some-time Squeeze member Jools Holland on piano. Clapton played some outstanding guitar on Ben E. King's classic 'Stand By Me', Spandau Ballet's 'Through The Barricades' as well as his own performance of 'Wonderful Tonight' and 'Behind the Mask'.

If last year's highlight had been the appearance of ex-Beatle Paul McCartney, this year's was doubly so with George Harrison and Ringo Starr turning up. George performed his 'While My Guitar Gently Weeps' with Clapton contributing an almost exact copy of the sweet solo he had done on the original version back at Abbey Road Studios in 1968. Ringo ended the evening by singing 'With A Little Help

■ SET LIST ■

Wembley Arena, London, 5th/6th June 1987,
Prince's Trust concerts

Running In The Family (*Mark King*) • If I was (*Midge Ure*) • Wonderful Tonight (*Eric Clapton*) • Behind The Mask (*Eric Clapton*) • Stand By Me (*Ben E King*) • You've Lost That Lovin' Feelin' (*Phil Collins and Paul Young*) • Through The Barricades (*Spandau Ballet*) • Your Song (*Elton John*) • Saturday Night's All Right For Fighting (*Elton John*) • While My Guitar Gently Weeps (*George Harrison*) • Here Comes The Sun (*George Harrison*) • It's The Same Old Song (*Phil Collins and Paul Young*) • I Can't Help Myself (*Phil Collins and Paul Young*) • Reach Out I'll Be There (*Phil Collins and Paul Young*) • With A Little Help From My Friends (*Ringo Starr and all the evening's performers*)

Jamming with Buddy Guy in Chicago, with Sugar Blue on harp in the background

Lionel Richie with Eric guesting, at the special Princes Trust concert at Wembley in 1987, in front of the Prince and Princess of Wales

From My Friends' with all the evening's performers on stage and which featured yet another great solo.

In July Clapton was again in the public eye when he turned up to play a version of his 1974 hit of Bob Marley's 'I Shot The Sheriff' for Island Records' 25th Birthday Party at Pinewood Studios. He was now also devoting a lot of his spare time to a lifelong passion, cricket. Eric had always liked the game from his childhood in Ripley when most of his idols would be the village cricketers. Even when he became a professional musician he would still check the big match scores. His present involvement came about when he was introduced to leading player Ian Botham in 1984

at a Test Match between England and the West Indies. The two found they had a lot in common and became good friends. In fact, towards the end of 1986, he gave Ian his Ferrari red prototype Fender Stratocaster after having been given the cricket bat Ian had done so well with in Australia.

Eric would go and see his friend play when possible and even formed an Eric Clapton XI made up of various music and film celebrities for charity games. He had already played in matches in Ripley and Finchley in 1986 and decided to make it more official by having badges, blazers and jumpers made up with the team logo showing a guitar crossed with a

Not quite the wizz with a cricket bat as with a guitar, Eric is bowled out during an all-star charity match. Behind the wicket, England player David Capel

cricket bat on a purple background. Eric also got involved in a project by The Bunburys — actually the Bee Gees with special guests — based on children's cartoon characters depicting cricketing rabbits that were illustrated by Jan Brychta with stories by David English. David was a friend of Clapton's from the RSO days and saw The Bunburys as a way of promoting cricket in state school education.

In fact, Barry Gibb and David English wrote a song called 'Fight' for Eric which he recorded for the project and was released in 1988 partly to support boxer Frank Bruno who was to fight Mike Tyson for the heavyweight championship of the world. The rarely seen video featured cartoon characters of Clapton, Botham, who sang back-up vocals, and the Gibb brothers. An album was recorded with special guests George Harrison and Elton John, but has so far eluded release.

In July, B.B.C. Radio One broadcast a six-part series titled 'Behind The Mask' which traced Clapton's life and career to date. Each programme lasted an hour and featured interviews with his family as well as past and present musical associates such as Phil Collins, Mark Knopfler, George Harrison and Jack

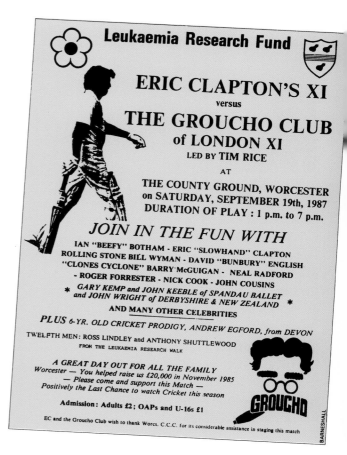

Bruce. The series was essential listening for the guitarist's fans although it offered little or no new information or rare musical items.

In September he flew to New York and into controversy. He had accepted to do a television and poster advertisement for Michelob beer, which for an ex-alcoholic seemed a curious decision. To make matters worse, Clapton had actually started drinking again, although it was only evident to close friends and band members. But to make such an advert at this time seemed contradictory. As its soundtrack he re-recorded J.J. Cale's 'After Midnight' and in the television ad could be seen playing it live on stage in a night club with a voice-over stating 'The night belongs to Michelob'. At no stage, however, did it say Eric Clapton drank the stuff!

The club where it was filmed was called the Lone Star Cafe and in the evening Clapton caught the excellent Roomfull Of Blues band performing there. He of course seized the opportunity to jam with them and their incredible lead guitarist Ronnie Earl, who incidentally has since left the band to form Ronnie Earl And The Broadcasters.

After the shoot, Clapton returned home only to find himself in front of more cameras. This time it was to film a special club appearance of him playing with Buddy Guy for inclusion in the aforementioned 'South Bank Show' television programme due for broadcast in December. The event took place at Ronnie Scott's club in Soho on 6 October and although only half an hour of material was filmed, Buddy and Eric played for over two hours while the cameras were being reloaded. Numbers performed included 'Stormy Monday', 'Worried Life Blues', 'Key To The Highway' and some instrumentals.

Three days later Eric again joined Buddy at Dingwalls and they played 'The Things I Used To Do', 'My Time After A While', 'Going Down', 'Sweet Sixteen' and 'Stormy Monday' among others. Jeff Beck, who was in the audience, was due to join them for the encore, but unfortunately had to leave early as the show went on longer than planned.

At the end of October Clapton started an Australian and Japanese tour with Nathan East on bass, Steve Ferrone on drums and Alan Clark, from Dire Straits, on keyboards who had replaced Greg

At the Tex-Mex Lone Star Cafe in New York, jamming with the sensational Ronnie Earl of Roomful of Blues

Eric in full flight during the
U.K. television special filmed
at Ronnie Scott's Club for the
'South Bank Show'

Phillinganes who was now playing on Michael Jackson's 'Bad' world tour. The last date of the tour itinerary was at the Castle Hall in Osaka, Japan on 9 November.

In December the 'South Bank Show' television special was at long last broadcast. Among the highlights of the documentary were footage of Eric Clapton and Jack Bruce playing Cream songs on Eric's patio, previously unseen footage from the near-legendary *Rolling Hotel* film, portions of the Ronnie Scott's show with Buddy Guy and an interview with the man himself. Typically, Eric ended the year by playing a small show at the village hall, Dunsfold, with Gary Brooker, Andy Fairweather-Low and Henri Spinetti.

SILVER JUBILEE

Early in January Clapton began rehearsals for the now-traditional Royal Albert Hall shows in London which were preceded by two warm-up shows at the N.E.C. in Birmingham.

Buddy Guy and Clapton became regular jamming partners over the years. Most of this two-hour session at Ronnie Scott's was not even filmed, let alone ending up on the cutting room floor!

Eric and bass player Nathan East during a Tokyo date in November 1987

Wife Patti was the inspiration for Eric's two most famous love songs, 'Layla' and 'Wonderful Tonight'

The band he had used for the Australian and Japanese dates was now augmented by Katie Kissoon and Tessa Niles on backing vocals, Ray Cooper on percussion and, for the second year running, Mark Knopfler on guitar.

This year was special for Eric Clapton as it celebrated 25 years on the road. A special silver programme was sold at all his concerts throughout the world and was to prove very popular, selling out at each show and now commanding a high price among fans. The only disappointment was a near-repetition of the previous year's set, mainly due to the fact that there was no new material out. His last release had been a retrospective album, *The Cream Of Eric Clapton* which had come out to tie in with Christmas.

After the Albert Hall concerts he played at the Civic Hall in Guildford where he was joined by Elton John and Phil Collins. The concerts lasted for more than two hours, although in Birmingham the version of 'Same Old Blues' was somewhat tedious lasting 25 minutes and featuring solos by all band members. By the time they had reached London it was reduced to a more economical 10 minutes.

Towards the end of March, Clapton recorded a track with Anne Dudley for the robbery scene in Phil Collin's *Buster* film. He was not credited but the track appears on the sountrack album. Similar in style to his work on 'Edge Of Darkness', his playing was perfectly suited to the scene.

Polygram released an amazing retrospective in April to celebrate his 25th anniversary, entitled *Crossroads*. The boxed set traced his career from the Yardbirds' first demos right through to 1987's re-recording of 'After Midnight' and sandwiched in between are some of his greatest numbers including 'Cocaine', 'Layla', 'Wonderful Tonight' and a wealth of unreleased material. The package was lovingly put together by Bill Levinson and is a great tribute to a great artist.

At the end of April Clapton did some more soundtrack work. This time it was for Mickey Rourke's film *Homeboy* and was to feature very varied work from Eric including some fine dobro playing. He spent a week at Townhouse Studios for the recording only to return there in early May to record some tracks for a Second World War documentary titled 'Peace In Our Time' for British television.

Mark Knopfler had asked Clapton to return the compliment and play with a reformed Dire Straits for the forthcoming 'Free Nelson Mandela' concert at Wembley Stadium. The two were also committed to appear at the Princes Trust concerts given at London's Royal Albert Hall, a few days before the Mandela concert. This show featured an array of top performers including Stevie Wonder, the Eurythmics, George Michael, Sting, Simple Minds and Tracy Chapman. The concert celebrated the 70th birthday of the world's most famous political prisoner and with a worldwide television audience of millions, it undoubtedly helped the already increasing pressure on the South African government to release him, which they subsequently did.

The Dire Straits set opened with a rumbustious

version of 'Walk Of Life' and featured some exceptional soloing from Clapton after which he mainly contributed rhythm guitar. However, he stepped out to sing one of the best versions of 'Wonderful Tonight' with some superb harmony vocals from Dire Straits. In fact, as a direct result of his appearance, *The Cream Of Eric Clapton* album shot up the charts once again.

The two Prince's Trust concerts featured the usual selection of current acts such as T'Pau, Wet Wet Wet and a supergroup consisting of Midge Ure on guitar and vocals, Howard Jones on keyboards, Queen's John Deacon and Brian May on bass and guitar respectively, the Phantom Horns, and Mark Brzezicki on drums. They backed the Bee Gees, Joe Cocker, Rick Astley, Phil Collins and Peter Gabriel. The headliner was billed as Eric Clapton and his Band with special friends. The line up consisted of Phil Collins and Steve Ferrone, Tessa Niles and Katie Kissoon on backing vocals, Mark Knopfler, Nathan East, Ray Cooper, Alan Clark on keyboards and Elton John on electric piano and vocals. This amazing outfit played 'Behind The Mask', an electrifying version of

Above and left: *Not since Live Aid had there been a rock spectacular like the ten-hour 1988 Nelson Mandela Concert in front of 80,000 Wembley fans and a TV audience of millions. Here is Clapton guesting with Mark Knopfler and Dire Straits*

In the gracious presence of their
Royal Highness
the Prince and Princess of Wales
(6th June)

THE
PRINCE'S TRUST

ROCK
GALA

SUNDAY 5th &
MONDAY 6th JUNE

THE
ROYAL
ALBERT
HALL

● RICK ASTLEY

● PAT BENATAR

● ERIC CLAPTON
& HIS BAND

● JOE COCKER

● PHIL COLLINS

● FOUR TOPS

● T'PAU

● WET WET WET

THE PRINCE'S TRUST ALL-STAR BAND
M.D. MIDGE URE

Tickets: £25, £20, £15 on sale from 10 am Sat. 30th April from
Albert Hall, Keith Prowse & usual agents (subject to booking fee)
By post from Prince's Trust, P.O. Box 2, London W6 0LQ
Cheques payable to Prince's Trust Box Office, enclose SAE
CREDIT CARD HOTLINE 01 741 8989
Maximum 4 tickets per person.

Above: Among Eric's 'special friends' for the 1988 Prince's Trust Gala was Elton John

Right: Rick Wills, Mike Rutherford and Clapton during the open-air charity event at Wintershall, July 1988

'Cocaine', 'Money For Nothing', 'I Don't Wanna Go On With You Like That' and 'Layla'. This was definitely the highlight of the two evenings with the fans on their feet from the first note. As an encore they were joined by all the evening's performers with Joe Cocker leading them through his inimitable version of Lennon and McCartney's 'With A Little Help From My Friends'.

Another special occasion happened on the evening of 6 June. Eric was presented by Prince Charles with a model of a silver Fender Stratocaster mounted on a small plinth, to commemorate Eric's

25th anniversary in the music business. The whole concert from 6 June was broadcast on American radio and the highlights were also released on video.

Towards the end of June Eric co-produced with Rob Fraboni three tracks for Davina McCall as well as contributing a guitar solo or two. The sessions have yet to see the light of day.

On 2 July Eric was invited to play at a special charity concert at Wintershall in Surrey. The impressive line up consisted of Gary Brooker, Andy Fairweather-Low, Phil Collins, Howard Jones, Mike Rutherford on guitar, Rick Wills on bass, Jody Linscott on percussion, Henry Spinetti, Frank Mead and Mel Collins on saxes, Vicky Brown, Sam Brown and Carol Kenyon on backing vocals. They played for two and a half hours to a very enthusiastic crowd who were fortunate enough to attend this special event in aid of the King Edward VII Hospital.

The guests were decked out in evening dress and had arrived when it was still daylight and began setting up tables in the picnic area for a good view of the lakeside stage. Picnic baskets were opened to reveal lavish feasts as champagne corks popped. The

select audience was treated to such covers as 'Celebrate', and 'You Can't Hurry Love' in addition to well-known hits by the musicians present including 'Wide Eyed And Legless', 'No One Is To Blame', 'Abacab', 'Whiter Shade Of Pale', 'I Want To Know What Love Is', 'Behind The Mask', 'Cocaine'and 'It's In The Way That You Use It'. Well into the concert many of the well-heeled crowd had kicked off their evening shoes and were dancing barefoot on the grass. Clapton was in fine form contributing one stunning guitar solo after another.

He took a well-deserved break from the seemngly endless round of charity bashes before rehearsing for a long North American tour that started on 1 September at the Starplex Amphitheater in Dallas, Texas. Mark Knopfler came along for the trip as did percussionist Jody Linscott. It was the first chance for American audiences to catch this line-up and reviews were generally very positive. As usual, Clapton took the opportunity to jam whenever possible and joined Elton John onstage at the Hollywood Bowl in Los Angeles for a lively version of 'Saturday Night's Alright For Fighting'; he also jammed with the newly reformed Little Feat on their classic 'Apolitical Blues', in the same city.

The last date of the tour was at the Copps Coliseum in Hamilton, Ontario, on 8 October and Eric joined his support group Buckwheat Zydeco for a version of Derek And The Dominos's 'Why Does Love Got To Be So Sad'. He had contributed a guitar solo earlier in the year to the same track on Buckwheat's *Taking It Home* album.

Clapton went to New York after the tour and participated in a historic jam session with Jack Bruce on 11 October at the Bottom Line Club in New York for two Cream classics, 'Spoonful', which lasted for 16 minutes, and 'Sunshine Of Your Love'. He used a Penza Sohr guitar lent to him by Pat Thrall, Jack's guitarist. Listening to the tapes suggests that a Cream reformation might not be such a good idea unless some new life can be breathed into those old numbers. To be fair, however, they had not rehearsed and it was a totally spontaneous event.

At the end of October, Clapton undertook a special four-date tour of Japan with Mark Knopfler and Elton John. One concert took place at the huge Tokyo Dome which was later broadcast on both Japanese radio and television. It was interesting to

on 28 November. The event took place at a special charity auction organized by Beck's ex-girlfriend Celia Hammond.

Clapton ended the year on a festive note by turning up to play at Gary Brooker's now-annual 'knees-up' at the Dunsfold village hall on 23 December alongside Gary, Andy Fairweather-Low, Henry Spinetti, Boz Burrell on bass and Frank Mead on sax. Numbers played included 'Lead Me To The Water', 'I Feel Good', 'It's A Man's World', 'You Can't Judge A Book By Its Cover' and 'Whiter Shade Of Pale'. Eric played his favourite 'Blackie' guitar for this special show.

As well as turning up at a Womack And Womack show at Dingwalls in Camden Town on 10 January on which he ended up playing two numbers, Eric Clapton began 1990 rehearsing with two bands for his forthcoming British tour. On the first part of the tour the four-piece band would appear, with Phil Collins, Nathan East, and the return of Greg Phillinganes who had completed his engagement for Michael Jackson. The second half consisted of the big band with Steve Ferrone replacing Collins, Mark Knopfler, Tessa Niles

*Although busy by any standards, Eric was able to assume a more relaxed attitude (**above**) in many ways – as long as 'relaxed' included gigging, sessions and the occasional jam like the one (**right**) involving Bobby Womack at London's Dingwall's Club*

hear Eric's guitar on Elton's numbers giving them an extra dimension, particularly on the slower songs.

Clapton returned to New York in early December for a week's recording for a new Carole King album at Skyline Studios. The two numbers he played on were 'City Streets' and 'Ain't That The Way'. Eric's drummer Steve Ferrone also played on the session. During their stay in New York, they would often hang out at the China Club and relax after working in the studio.

On his return to England Clapton involved himself in another jam with former Jimi Hendrix Experience members Mitch Mitchell and Noel Redding as well as Jeff Beck at the Hard Rock Cafe in London

Nathan and Greg with
'Slowhand' during the '89
Albert Hall stint

and Katie Kissoon, Alan Clark, Ray Cooper and of course Nathan and Greg.

Both line-ups were equally effective in different ways. The quartet obliged Clapton to play more guitar than he would do in the big band, but the larger format was more powerful and possibly more entertaining for the crowds with Ray Cooper's antics and the stage camaraderie between Greg and Nathan and the rest of the band, particularly in 'Tearing Us Apart' which included a great dance routine.

The trip started in Sheffield at the City Hall on 16 January before moving on to Newcastle's City Hall, Edinburgh's Playhouse and London's Royal Albert Hall for a 12-night engagement, the last six being with the big band. On 25 January Clapton was interviewed by top television chat-show host Terry Wogan. Fame at last! Eric also participated in the filming for Carole King's new single 'City Streets' and asked her to come and sing on a couple of numbers at the Albert Hall. She joined him for 'After Midnight' and 'Can't Find My Way Home'.

After the London shows he recorded the title music for the new James Bond film *Licence To Kill* but this remains unreleased due to a disagreement

Never noted for the leather
look, Eric donned biker
trousers and 'beetle-crusher'
shoes to match for one of the
Royal Albert Hall shows

between the producers of the Bond films and Clapton's management company.

Most of February was spent searching for suitable songs for recording for a new album. Clapton's songwriting had dried up and he had to rely on other people's material. Studio time was booked throughout March and April at New York's Power Station and Skyline Studios for both his new album and the soundtrack for *Lethal Weapon 2*.

The soundtrack work was in fact superior to the previous *Lethal Weapon* and consisted of some exhilarating interplay between Clapton and saxophonist David Sanborn. Eric's playing in the studio had finally taken on the same confidence shown in concert. Recording sessions now involved a more mature Eric Clapton choosing material that suited him and playing accordingly. He surrounded himself with a strong team of musician friends including Robert Cray who played on several tracks as well as co-writing the beautifully haunting 'Old Love' with Eric. Another old friend who offered his services was George Harrison who played on 'That Kind Of Woman' and 'Run So Far'.

Clapton also played guitar on a couple of notable

The twelve record breaking shows at the Royal Albert Hall in 1990 spotlighted every facet of Clapton's music. The masked drummer (**left**) with Greg, Eric and Nathan is Phil Collins, while (**below**) the big band takes a bow – Tessa Niles, Mark Knopfler, Ray Cooper, Katie Kissoon, Steve Ferone, Clapton, Greg and Nathan

Carl Perkins is joined by Eric during his two-show engagement at New York's Bottom Line

During May 1989, Clapton presented an award, for a change, rather than being the recipient. It was an honourary Songwriters Hall of Fame award to the late Roy Orbison which Eric presented to Roy's widow Barbara; the two are seen here on the way to the CBS TV studios in Los Angeles where the ceremony was recorded

sessions. One was for Cyndi Lauper on a track called 'Insecurious', the other for Italian superstar Zucchero Sugar Fornaciari on a track called 'A Wonderful World'.

Producer Russ Titelman brought out the best in Clapton resulting in his most coherent album to date. A further track was recorded at the Townhouse Studios in London called 'Bad Love' that he co-wrote with Mick Jones of Foreigner. The idea was to produce an obvious single which it certainly was.

Overdubs and mixing took place in New York in May. That month Eric also took the opportunity of playing a set on 9 May with his old friend Carl Perkins at the Bottom Line club in New York, running through 'Mean Woman Blues', 'Matchbox', 'Roll Over Beethoven', 'Maybelline', 'Whole Lotta Shakin'', 'Hound Dog', 'Blue Suede Shoes' and 'Goin' Down The Road Feeling Bad'.

At the end of May, Clapton attended the first Elvis Awards ceremony at the Armoury in New York and was presented by Keith Richards with an award for best guitarist. He also played on the obligatory jam session which took place at the end of the evening for a ten minute version of 'I Hear You Knockin''

Keef'n'Eric *(above)* front the all-star jam at the Elvis Awards in New York, after Clapton received the Best Guitarist trophy *(left)* from his Rolling Stone buddy

alongside Richards, Dave Edmunds, Jeff Healey, Tina Turner, Clarence Clemons, Vernon Reid and many others.

Another all-star jam took place at Wintershall in Surrey on 1 July when Clapton once again joined the 'Band Du Lac' as they were jokingly called because of the stage's location at the foot of the lake. This year the band comprised Gary Brooker, Andy Fairweather-Low, Henry Spinetti, Stevie Winwood, Mike Rutherford, Phil Collins, Frank Mead and Mel Collins, Dave Bronze on bass and Sam and Vicky Brown on vocals.

JOURNEYMAN

Clapton started a tour a week later that would take him to Holland, Switzerland, Israel and Africa. Guitarist Phil Palmer had now joined the line-up and added his distinctive style to the repertoire. Palmer had been Paul Brady's guitarist and had met Eric when he played on a session for Paul a few years back. He is also a prolific session player turning up on albums by artists as diverse as Joan Armatrading and George Michael. The set for the tour was almost identical to the big band's at the Albert Hall. The highlight of the trip was the last date on 30 July at the Machava National Stadium in Maputo, Mozambique in front of an estimated audience of over 100,000 people. All proceeds went to a local housing project.

On his return to England Clapton started a round of promotional interviews for various magazines, newspapers, radio and television. He also participated in a concert at Da Campo Boario in Rome with his friend Zucchero Sugar Fornaciari on 28 September. The whole concert was broadcast on Italian television and featured other guest artists including Paul Young, Clarence Clemons and Dee Dee Bridgewater. Zucchero is huge in Italy, outselling Springsteen, Madonna and Prince and is best described as a cross between Joe Cocker and Bruce Springsteen. Eric played and sang on 'A Wonderful World'; he had played on the studio version earlier in the year.

Shortly after, he flew to New York again for more promotional work and to film a video for 'Pretending' in Los Angeles. He also took the chance to jump up on stage to play with friends in New York — Elton John at Madison Square Garden and the Rolling Stones at Shea Stadium. On both occasions the crowd went wild as he added his distinctive guitar solos to Elton's 'Rocket Man' and 'Little Red Rooster' with the Stones.

In Los Angeles he once again played with the Rolling Stones at the Coliseum for another version of 'Little Red Rooster'. He spent the next two days filming the video for his forthcoming single before returning to New York for an appearance on a David Sanborn television special on 25 October where he played 'Hard Times', 'Old Love' which also featured Robert Cray, and 'Before You Accuse Me'. This was the first airing of new numbers from his next album *Journeyman*.

He flew home the next day. Clapton's next public appearance was on Sue Lawley's television chat show 'Saturday Matters' on 28 October. He was interviewed along with Pete Townshend and they also played a beautiful version of Muddy Waters' 'Standin' Around Cryin'' on acoustic guitars.

Eric's new album *Journeyman* was released in

On the road again; Eric and percussionist Ray Cooper at the Grand Hotel Dolder, Zurich, Switzerland (**left**), and jamming with the 'Stones at the Shea Stadium (**below**)

Clapton at the time of the
release of the multi-platinum
album Journeyman, at the end
of 1989

During the American tour in the Fall of '89, Eric also managed to squeeze in a TV show with sax star David Sanborn, seen here in the background on the right

While in the 'States, Eric attended the opening of an exhibition of pictures by Sixties photographer Michael Cooper; also at the show, John Mayall (left) Bill Wyman and Al Cooper

November to worldwide critical acclaim. These days no longer a songwriter, the material he chose suited him perfectly. On 18 November he played unannounced at a special charity show on behalf of a body called Parents For Safe Food at the Royal Albert Hall in London. He played an eight-minute version of 'Edge Of Darkness' with Carl Davis and his Organic Symphony Orchestra. It was an amazing sight to see and hear and was a preview of three nights with the National Philharmonic Orchestra that would take place the following February.

In early December, Clapton continued his hectic schedule by recording the title music for the film *Communion* along with some incidental music. The sessions once again took place at the Townhouse Studios in London's Shepherds Bush.

No sooner had he finished the recording that he once again flew out to New York. Upon arrival, he went straight down to Atlantic City in New Jersey. The Rolling Stones were finishing their hugely successful 'Steel Wheels' tour of America with three nights at the Convention Center and decided to invite some special guests to help them celebrate the end of the tour. Clapton appeared on 19 December to play a couple of immaculate solos on 'Rooster' which had Jagger and Richards smiling with approval. He stayed on stage for John Lee Hooker's spot on 'Boogie Chilun'. The other guests had been Axl and Izzy from Guns N' Roses on 'Salt Of The Earth'. The whole show was broadcast live on pay television with a simultaneous stereo broadcast on various radio stations across the States. It was without a doubt the best show of the tour and with an audience of only 16,000 it was the smallest venue of the tour.

On his return home Eric played with Gary Brooker's No Stiletto Shoes at Chiddingfold's Ex-Servicemen's Club on 23 December. This was one of those relaxing enjoyable low-key jams with friends where he can be just a back-up guitarist without the pressure of being in front of a huge crowd.

The year started with rehearsals for Clapton's most ambitious series of concerts. He decided to perform in four different musical settings ranging from straight blues to orchestral events with the National Philharmonic Orchestra. The plan was to perform four different sets with four different line-ups. The small group line-up was a quartet of Eric with Steve Ferrone on drums, Nathan East on bass

and Greg Phillinganes on keyboards. For the 'big-band' sound he added Phil Palmer on guitar, Alan Clark, Ray Cooper, Katie Kissoon/Tessa Niles on vocals, and a horn section comprising Ronnie Cuber, Randy Brecker, Louis Marini and Alan Rubin. For a series of 'blues nights' he chose guitarists Robert Cray and Buddy Guy, Robert Cousins on bass, Johnnie Johnson on piano and making a welcome return to the

■ SET LIST ■

Albert Hall, London, 1990
Set list for 4 piece and 13 piece:

Pretending • Running On Faith • Breaking Point • I Shot The Sheriff • White Room • Can't Find My Way Home • Bad Love • Lay Down Sally • Before You Accuse Me • No Alibis • Old Love • Tearing Us Apart • Wonderful Tonight • Cocaine • Layla • Crossroads • Sunshine Of Your Love

Set list for blues nights:

Key To The Highway • Worried Life Blues • All Your Love • Watch Yourself • Standing Around Crying • Long Distance Call • Johnnie's Boogie • Going Down Slow • You Belong To Me • Cry For Me • Howlin' For My Baby • Same Thing • Money • Five Long Years • Something On Your Mind • Every Thing Gonna Be Alright • Sweet Home Chicago • My Time After A While • Wee Wee Baby

Set list for orchestra nights:

Crossroads • Bell Bottom Blues • Lay Down Sally • Holy Mother • I Shot The Sheriff • Hard Times • Can't Find My Way Home • Edge Of Darkness • Old Love • Wonderful Tonight • White Room • Concerto For Electric Guitar And Orchestra • Layla • Sunshine Of Your Love

drums, Jamie Oldaker. The fourth line up consisted of the big band without the horns but with the huge orchestral forces of the National Philharmonic.

The tour started with the four piece at the N.E.C. in Birmingham for three nights on 14–16 January before breaking all records at London's Albert Hall by playing no fewer than 18 nights at the famous venue. In between the shows the four piece appeared on B.B.C. television's 'Wogan' show playing a version of the new single 'Bad Love'.

At long last the set had changed with the a large chunk of *Journeyman* being performed. The show opened with 'Pretending' giving Eric plenty of opportunity to use his wah-wah pedal which he did at regular intervals throughout the performance. The shows in London were divided into six nights of the four piece, six of the 13-piece, three with the blues band and three with the orchestra.

The last night of each format was recorded and filmed for possible release in November 1990. BBC Radio One also broadcast two complete concerts live nationwide: the opening blues night on 3 February and the middle orchestral night on 9 February.

Left and Below: The Blues Nights at the Royal Albert Hall in 1990 were of special significance to Eric, delving into his musical roots with fellow masters of the blues Buddy Guy and Robert Cray

Above: Another of the unique occasions at the 1990 Albert Hall Concerts were the orchestral evenings with the National Philharmonic Orchestra

As soon as the season was over, the band went on tour (*above right*), and seen here taking a bow at Madison Square Garden (*right*)

Most extraordinary were the orchestral nights, which were very grandiose. Wearing an evening jacket and using just a small amp, Clapton played beautifully. Not every number worked as well as others in this environment, but some actually took on a brand new lease of life. 'Bell Bottom Blues' from the Derek And The Dominos period was quite superb as was 'Holy Mother', originally from the *August* album. 'Edge Of Darkness' retained its original power but played live with a full orchestra it had an added spine-tingling quality. The climax of these evenings was the performance of 'Concerto For Electric Guitar And Orchestra' which had been specificaly composed for Clapton by Michael Kamen.

After the English dates, he and his band went off on a 13-date tour of Europe and Scandinavia. The set was the same as the London shows and was received enthusiastically by fans. In The Hague, Billy Preston came on for a jam.

Towards the end of March, they flew out to the United States to rehearse for a tour that would occupy most of the year. They also played on the popular 'Saturday Night Live' television show performing 'No Alibis', 'Pretending' and 'Wonderful Tonight'. As the credits rolled Eric could be seen and heard playing 'Born Under A Bad Sign' with the house band. In fact after the cameras had stopped rolling they played a 20-minute set comprising the aforementioned number and 'Hideaway'.

A few guests dropped in at various shows including Daryl Hall at Madison Square Garden, Stevie Ray Vaughan in Detroit and George Harrison at the L.A. Forum in Los Angeles. The first part of the tour ended at the Shoreline Amphitheater on 5 May. The following day Eric and his band appeared at the New York Armoury for the Elvis awards performing 'Before You Accuse Me'. At the end of the show he was presented with a Living Legend Award by Buddy Guy before all the celebrities got up and jammed on 'Sweet Home Chicago'. Other than Clapton's band, the all-star line-up included Bo Diddley, Lou Reed, Dave Stewart and Buddy Guy.

Clapton left for Antigua for a break before coming home to play the special Nordoff–Robbins charity

The 1990 Elvis Awards line-up, including Bo Diddley (with the rectangular guitar), Lou Reed, Buddy Guy and Eurythmics' Dave Stewart

Right: Congratulations all round; Eric and bass player Nathan East at the Elvis Awards

Far right: Clapton in San Diego, 1990

Below: Tragically, the last appearance of Stevie Ray Vaughan (far left) with Phil Packer, brother Jimmy Vaughan, Buddy Guy and Eric

Left: *Eric's American performances in 1990 set the seal on a year of triumphs*

concert at Knebworth. This was *the* concert of 1990 with a bill including Paul McCartney, Pink Floyd, Status Quo, Genesis and Robert Plant.

At the end of July Eric returned to the U.S. to complete the second part of the tour that would last until 15 August. Two shows at the Alpine Valley in East Troy were very special with Jeff Healey, Jimmie and Stevie Ray Vaughan, Buddy Guy and Robert Cray jamming on the encore of 'Sweet Home Chicago'. It was after this show on the 26 August, that Stevie Ray was killed in a tragic helicopter accident along with three members of Eric's personal entourage, Bobby Brooks, Nigel Browne and Colin Smythe-Park. The loss of the popular Texan guitarist was a real blow to American blues-rock music.

In late September 1990 Eric made his first professional visit to South America, to be greeted with the same enthusiasm he now enjoys worldwide, followed by sell-out tours of Australia, Asia and Japan.

In February 1991 another record-breaking season of 24 nights at the Royal Albert Hall have meant a higher profile for Eric Clapton than at any time during an eventful and artistically distinguished career.

Los Angeles '90: some of Clapton's most enthusiastic audiences have been on West Coast dates

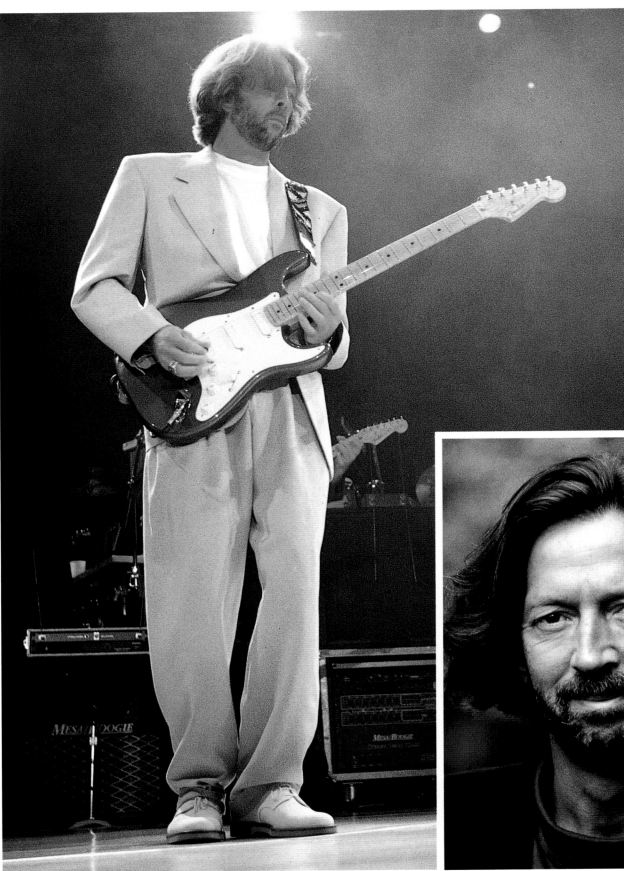

It was a year that would culminate in new pastures in South America, followed by the well-tested audiences in Japan – a lead-up for Eric to another Albert Hall marathon early in 1991. American fans, as at Sand Diego (left), still form the backbone of Clapton's immense following, along with his fans on home territory.

■ D I S C O G R A P H Y

SINGLES
Behind The Mask (*Mosdell, Sakamoto, Jackson*)
Grand Illusion
U.K. Duck W8461
Sunset Sound Studios, Los Angeles
April–May 1986
Prod. Phil Collins
Released January 1987

It's In The Way That You Use It (*Clapton, Robertson*)
Bad Influence (*Cray, Vannice*)
U.K. Duck W8397
Surrey Sounds Studios, Leatherhead, U.K.
September 1986
Sunset Sound Studios, Los Angeles
April–May 1986
Prod. Tom Dowd/Phil Collins
Released August 1987

Holy Mother (*Clapton, Bishop*)
Tangled In Love (*Levy, Feldman*)
U.K. Duck W8141
Sunset Sound Studios, Los Angeles
April 1986
Air Studios, Montserrat
April 1984
Prod. Phil Collins
Released November 1987

Tearing Us Apart (*Clapton, Phillinganes*)
Hold On (Clapton, Collins)

U.K. Duck W8299
Sunset Sound Studios, Los Angeles
April–May 1986
Prod. Phil Collins
Released June 1987

Bad Love (*Clapton/Jones*)
Before You Accuse Me (*McDaniel*)
U.K. Duck W2644
Power Station Studios, NYC/ Skyline Studios NYC/Townhouse Studios, London
March–May 1989
Prod. Russ Titelman
Released January 1990

No Alibis (*Williams*)
Running On Faith (*Williams*)
U.K. Duck W9981
Power Station Studios NYC/ Skyline Studios NYC
March–May 1989
Prod. Russ Titelman
Released March 1990

Pretending (*Williams*)
Hard Times (*Charles*)
U.K. Duck W9770
Power Sation Studios NYC/ Skyline Studios NYC
March–May 1989
Prod. Russ Titelman
Released June 1990

ALBUMS
AUGUST
It's In The Way That You Use It (*Clapton, Robertson*), **Run** (*Dozier*) **Tearing Us Apart** (*Clapton, Phillinganes*), **Bad Influence** (*Cray, Vannice*), **Walk Away** (*Levy, Feldman*), **Hung Up On Your Love** (*Dozier*), **Take A Chance** (*Clapton, Phillinganes, East*), **Hold On** (*Clapton, Collins*), **Miss You** (*Clapton, Phillinganes, Columby*), **Holy Mother** (*Clapton, Bishop*), **Behind The Mask** (*Mosdell, Sakamoto, Jackson*)
U.K. Duck WX71
Sunset Sound Studios, Los Angeles
April–May 1986
Surrey Sound Studios, Leatherhead U.K.
September 1986
Prod. Phil Collins/Tom Dowd
Released November 1986

JOURNEYMAN
Pretending (*Williams*), **Anything For Your Love** (*Williams*), **Bad Love** (*Clapton, Jones*), **Running On Faith** (*Williams*), **Hard Times** (*Charles*), **Hound Dog** (*Leiber, Stoller*), **No Alibis** (*Williams*), **Run So Far** (*Harrison*), **Old Love** (*Clapton, Cray*), **Breaking Point** (*Williams, Grebb*), **Lead Me On** (*Womack, Womack*), **Before You Accuse Me** (*McDaniel*)
U.K. Duck WX322
Power Station NYC, Skyline Studios NYC, Townhouse London
March–May 1989
Prod. Russ Titelman
Released November 1989

WEMBLEY ARENA

THE PRINCE'S TRUST
'76 BIRTHDAY PARTY '86
Friday, 20th June, '86 at 7.30 pm

GRAND TIER SOUTH
£5.00

PLUS £20.00 VOLUNTARY DONATION
TO BE RETAINED
See conditions on back

JUNE
20
1986

ENTER AT SOUTH DOOR ENTRANCE
77
ROW
C
SEAT
123

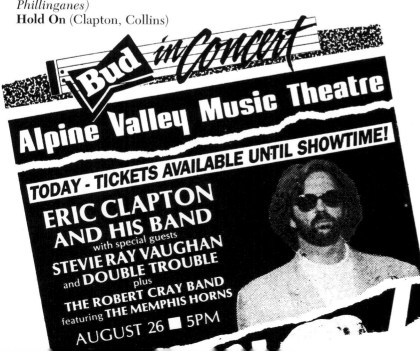

Bud in Concert

Alpine Valley Music Theatre
TODAY - TICKETS AVAILABLE UNTIL SHOWTIME!
ERIC CLAPTON AND HIS BAND
with special guests
STEVIE RAY VAUGHAN and DOUBLE TROUBLE
plus
THE ROBERT CRAY BAND
featuring THE MEMPHIS HORNS
AUGUST 26 ■ 5PM

■ TOURS

1987
January
26th Palatrussardi, Milan
29th Palaeur, Rome
30th Palapsort, Florence

1988
June
6th Evening concerts at Royal Albert Hall for Prince's Trust
8th/9th Dire Straits Show at The Odeon, Hammersmith
11th Dire Straits Show at Wembley Stadium
July
2nd Charity Show (Gary Brooker) Wintershall
September
1st Starplex Ampitheatre, Dallas, Texas
2nd Lakefront Arena, New Orleans, Louisanna 4th Civic Arena, Pittsburgh, Pennsylvania 6th Meadowlands Arena, Rutherford, New Jersey 7th Spectrum, Philadelphia, Pennsylvania 8th Capitol Center, Largo Maryland 10th Civic Center, Hartford, Connecticut 11th Nassau Coliseum, Uniondale, New York 13th/14th

Great Woods, Boston, Massachusetts 16th Palace, Detroit, Michigan 17th Alpine Valley, Milwaukee, Wisconsin 19th Fiddlers Green, Denver, Colorado 21st Shoreline Ampitheatre, San Francisco, California 22nd Arco Arena, Sacramento, California 23rd Irvine Meadows Ampitheatre, Laguna Hills California 26th Coliseum, Portland, Oregon 27th The Dome, Tacoma, Washington 28th P.N.E. Coliseum, Vancouver, British Columbia 30th Olympic Saddledome, Calgary, Alberta
October
1st Saskatchewan Place, Saskatoon, Saskatchewan 3rd The Arena, Winnepeg, Manitoba 4th Met. Centre, Minneapolis, Minnesota 6th Forum, Montreal, Quebec 7th Maple Leaf Gardens, Toronto, Ontario 8th Copps Coliseum, Hamilton, Ontario 31st Rainbow Hall, Nagoya, Japan
November
2nd The Dome, Tokyo 4th Budokan Theatre, Tokyo 5th The Stadium, Osaka

1989
U.K. TOUR
January
16th City Hall, Sheffield
17th City Hall, Newcastle
18th Playhouse, Edinburgh
20th–3rd February Royal Albert Hall, London
NETHERLANDS/SWISS/ ISRAELI/AFRICAN TOUR
July
6th/7th Statenhal, The Hague
9th/10th Hallenstadion, Zurich
13th Sultan's Pool Jerusalem 14th Zemach Amphitheatre, Sea of Galilee 15th/17th Caesarea Amphitheatre, Caesarea 22nd Somhlolo National Stadium, Swaziland 25th–26th Conference Centre, Harare, Zimbabwe 28th Boipuso Hall, Gaberone, Botswana 30th Machava National Stadium, Maputo, Swaziland

1990
U.K. TOUR
January
14th-16th N.E.C., Birmingham (4 piece)
18th/24th Royal Albert Hall, London (4 piece)
26th–3rd Feb Royal Albert Hall, London (13 piece)
February
3rd–5th Royal Albert Hall, London (blues band)
8th/9th/10th Royal Albert Hall, London (orchestra)
EUROPEAN TOUR
February
14th Icehall, Helsinki 16th The Glove, Stockholm 17th Skedsmo Hall, Oslo 19th KB Hall, Copenhagen 20th Sporthalle, Hamburg 22nd Forest National, Brussels 23rd Grugahalle, Essen 24th Statenhal, The Hague 26th–27th Palatrussardi, Milan
March
1st Olympiahalle, Munich
3rd/4th Zenith, Paris
5th Festhalle, Frankfurt
U.S.A. TOUR PART 1
March
28th The Omni, Atlanta
30th Coliseum, Charlotte, North Carolina

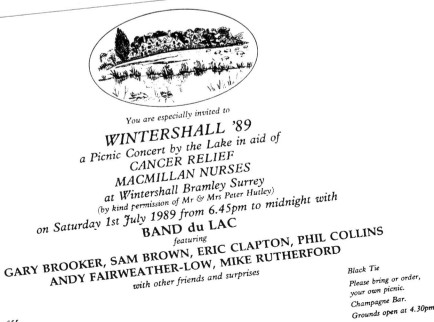

You are especially invited to
WINTERSHALL '89
a Picnic Concert by the Lake in aid of
CANCER RELIEF
MACMILLAN NURSES
at Wintershall Bramley Surrey
(by kind permission of Mr & Mrs Peter Hutley)
on Saturday 1st July 1989 from 6.45pm to midnight with
BAND du LAC
featuring
GARY BROOKER, SAM BROWN, ERIC CLAPTON, PHIL COLLINS ANDY FAIRWEATHER-LOW, MIKE RUTHERFORD
with other friends and surprises

Black Tie
Please bring or order,
your own picnic.
Champagne Bar.
Grounds open at 4.30pm

Tickets: £55
R.S.V.P. to:
Mrs Geraldine Lawson, Wintershall Estate Office,
Wintershall, Bramley, Surrey GU5 0LR

31st Dean Smith Centre, Chapel Hill, North Carolina
April
2nd Madison Square Garden, New York City **3rd** Meadowlands, Rutherford, New Jersey **4th** Spectrum, Philadelphia **6th** Nassau Coliseum, Uniondale, New York **7th** Carrier Dome, Syacuse, New York **9th/10th** Centrum, Worcester, Massachusetts **12th/13th** Civic Center, Hartford, Conneticut **15th** Palace of Aubern Hill, Detroit **16th** Riverfront Coliseum, Cincinnati, Ohio **17th** Richfield Coliseum, Buffalo NY **19th** Market Square Arena, Indianapolis **20th** Hilton Coliseum, Ames, Iowa **21st** The Arena, St. Louis, Missouri **23rd** Lakefront Arena, New Orleans **24th** The Summit, Houston, Texas **25th** Reunion Arena, Dallas, Texas
June
30th Knebworth

U.S.A. TOUR PART 2
July
23rd The Arena, Miami, Florida **25th** The Arena, Orlando, Florida **27th** Suncoast Dome, St. Petersburg, Florida **28th** Lakewood Amphitheatre, Atlanta, Georgia **30th** Starwood Amphitheatre, Nashville, Tennessee **31st** Mid-South Coliseum, Memphis, Tennessee
August
2nd The Coliseum, Gresnsboro, North Carolina **3rd–4th** Capitol Center, Washington D.C. **6th/7th** Meadowlands, East Rutherford, New Jersey **9th–11th** Great Woods, Mansfield, Massachusetts **13th** Saratoga P.A.C., Saratoga, New York **14th/15th** The Spectrum, Philadelphia, Pennsylvania **17th/18th** Nassau Coliseum, Uniondale, New York **21st** Blossom, Cleveland, Ohio **22nd** Pine Knob, Detroit, Michigan **23rd** Riverbend, Cincinnati, Ohio **25th/26th** Alpine Valley, East Troy, Wisconsin **28th** Sandstone Amphitheatre, Kansas City, Missouri **29th** The Arena, St.

Louis, Missouri **31st** Thompson-Bolling Arena, Knoxville, Tennessee
September
1st Oak Mountain Amphitheatre, Birmingham, Alabama
2nd Coast Coliseum, Biloxi, Mississippi

SOUTH AMERICAN TOUR
September
29th Estadio Nacional, Santiago, Chile
October
3rd Estadio Centemario, Montevideo, Uruguay **5th** Estadio River Plate, Buenos Aires, Argentina, **7th** Apoteus Square, Rio de Janeiro, Brazil **9th** Nilson Nelson, Brazilia, Brazil **11th** Mineirimo, Belo Horizonte, Brazil **13th** Orlando Scorpelli Stadium, Florianopolis, Brazil **16th** Gigantino, Porte Alegre, Brazil **21st** Olympia, Sao Paulo, Brazil

AUSTRALIAN TOUR
November
7th The Supertop, Auckland, New Zealand **10th** Royal Theatre, Canberra, Australia, **13th** Festival Theatre, Adelaide, Australia **15th** National Tennis Centre, Melbourne, Australia **17th** Entertainment Centre, Sidney, Australia **19th** Entertainment Centre, Brisbane, Australia

FAR EAST TOUR
November
24th Singapore
26th Kuala Lumpur
29th Honk Kong
December
4th–6th The Budokan, Tokyo **9th** Olympic Pool, Tokyo **10th** Rainbow Hall, Nagoya **11th** Castle Hill, Osaka **13th** The Arena, Yokohama

---

1991
January 31st–February 2nd
Dublin
February
5th–7th, 9th–11th Royal Albert Hall (4 piece)
13th–15th, 17th–19th RAH (9 piece)
23rd–25th, 27–March 1st RAH (blues)
March
3rd–5th, 7th–9th (orchestral)

HARVEY GOLDSMITH BY ARRANGEMENT WITH ROGER FORRESTER presents
ERIC CLAPTON AND HIS BAND
plus SPECIAL GUESTS
ROYAL ALBERT HALL
FRIDAY 29th
SATURDAY 30th
SUNDAY
FEBRUARY
3rd FEBRUARY
DAY 4th FEBRUARY
SOLD OUT
EXTRA SHOWS DUE TO PHENOMENAL DEMAND
MONDAY 25th JANUARY
TUESDAY 26th JANUARY
WEDNESDAY 27th JANUARY
7.30pm
Tickets £13.50 £11.50 £9.50 MAXIMUM 6 TICKETS PER PERSON
Tickets on sale over the counter from:
Royal Albert Hall Box Office Birmingham Odeon Nottingham Way Ahead
and Manchester Piccadilly Records

SESSION APPEARANCES

(albums unless otherwise stated)

Duane Allman Anthology
Jon Astley Everyone Loves The Pilot
Ashton, Gardner and Dyke The Worst Of

The Band The Last Waltz
The Beatles The Beatles
Marc Benno Lost In Austin
Stephen Bishop Careless; Red Cab To Manhattan; Bowling in Paris
Chuck Berry Hail Hail Rock'n'Roll
Gary Brooker Lead Me To The River; Echoes In The Night
Paul Brady Back To The Centre
Leona Boyd Labryinth

Jim Capaldi Some Come Running
Joe Cocker Stingray
Phil Collins Face Value But Seriously
The Crickets Rockin' 50s Rock'n'Roll
King Curtis Teasin' (*single*)

Roger Daltrey One Of The Boys
Rick Danko Rick Danko
Jesse Davis Jesse Davis
Gail Anne Dorsey Corporate World
Danny Douma Night Eyes
Doctor John Hollywood Be Thy Name; Sun, Moon and Herbs
Bob Dylan Desire; Hearts of Fire; Down In The Groove
Champion Jack Dupree From New Orleans To Chicago

Aretha Franklin Lady Soul

Kinky Friedman Lasso From El Paso

Bob Geldof Deep In The Heart Of Nowhere
Buddy Guy and Junior Wells Play The Blues

Corey Hart First Offence
George Harrison Wonderwall Music; All Things Must Pass; George Harrison; Cloud Nine

Michael Kamen Concerts For Saxophone And Orchestra
Bobby Keys Bobby Keys
Carol King City Streets
Freddie King Burglar; 1934–1976
Alexis Korner The Party Album

Corky Laing Makin' It In The Street
Ronnie Lane See Me
Ronnie Lane and Pete Townshend Rough Mix
Cyndi Lauper A Night To Remember
Jackie Lomax Is This What You Want
Arthur Louis First Album

John Martyn Glorious Fool
John Mayall Back To The Roots
Christine McVie Christine McVie

Yoko Ono Fly

Billy Preston Encouraging Words; That's The Way God Planned It

Lionel Richie Dancing On The Ceiling
Leon Russell Leon Russell; Leon Russel & the Shelter People

Soundtrack Buster; Back To The Future; Color of Money; Homeboy; Lethal Weapon; Lethal Weapon 2
Otis Spann The Blues of Otis Spann
Vivian Stanshall Labio Dental Fricative (*single*)
Ringo Starr Rotogravure; Old Wave
Stephen Stills Stephen Stills; '2'
Sting Nothing Like The Sun

Doris Troy Doris Troy
Tina Turner What You See Is What You Get (*12" single*); Live In Europe

Various Artists: Concert For BanglaDesh; Music From Free Creek; White Mansions; Secret Policeman's Other Ball; A Moment In Time
Martha Velez Fiends and Angels

Roger Waters Pros and Cons of Hitch Hiking
Bobby Whitlock Bobby Whitlock; Raw Velvet
The Who Tommy (*soundtrack*)
Howlin' Wolf The London Sessions; London Revisited

Zucchero Zucchero
Buckwheat Zydeco Taking It Home

CD SPECIALS

Previously unreleased tracks now available on CD

Goodbye Cream
(bonus track 'Anyone For Tennis')

EC Was Here
(full version of 'Drifting Blues')

No Reason To Cry
(extra track 'Last Night')

Backless
(full version of 'Early In The Morning')

August
(bonus track 'Grand Illusion')

MONO
2 COPIES.
SPOT PRODUCTIONS LIMITED
(CUSTOM DIVISION)
64 SOUTH MOLTON STREET
MAYFAIR LONDON W.1
TELEPHONE: GROSVENOR 7173-4-5
SPOT

Date		Client		
Job No.		ROBERT STIGWOOD		
		Programme CREAM L.P. SIDE II	REEL II OF II	
	Title	Timing	Title	Timing
1	CATSQUIRREL	8		
4	TILL LATE	9		
3	THE COFFEE SONG	10		
4	ROLLIN + A TUMBLIN	11		
5	I'm SO GLAD	12		
6	TOAD			

VITAL VIDEOS

Old Grey Whistle Test 1977
BBC Video

The Last Waltz 1976
Warner Bros. Video

Sweet Toronto 1969
Parkfield Video

Hail Hail Rock'n'Roll!!
CIC Video

Concert For Bangla Desh 1971
Warner Bros. Video

Tommy
RSO

Farewell Cream 1978
Channel 5 Video

ARMS
Channel 5 Video

Supershow 1969
Virgin Video

Alex Korner's 'Eat A Little Rhythm and Blues' 1978
BBC Video

Knebworth
Castle Music

The Cream of Eric Clapton
Polygram Video

Live 1985
Channel 5 Video

The Eric Clapton Concert
Radio Vision

'Alright Now' Island Records 25th Anniversary
Island Video

BB King and Friends
Video Collection

Rockabilly Session, Carl Perkins and Friends
Virgin Video

Eric Clapton The Man and His Music
Video Collection

Prince's Trust Birthday Party
Video Gems

Prince's Trust Rock Gala 1987
P.M.V.

Superstars In Concert
Telstar Video

Prince's Trust Rock Gala 1988
Video Collection

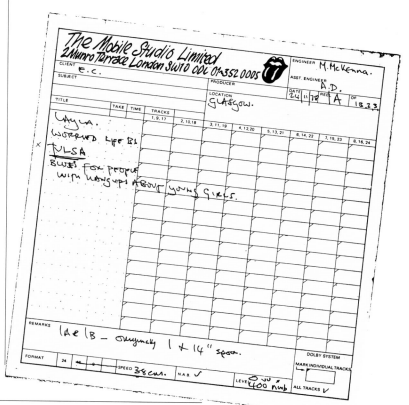

BEST OF THE BOOTLEGS

Eric Clapton's Cream
BBC sessions 1967–68 (*CD*)

The Legendary LA Forum Show
LA Forum, 1975 with Carlos Santana and Keith Moon (*double CD*)

Wonderful Tonight
Bremen, 1983 (*double LP*)

Behind The Sun Tour
NEC, Birmingham U.K. 1985 (*double LP*)

Rolling Stones 'Cocksucker Blues'
E.C. plays guitar on 'Brown Sugar'
(*Japanese CD*)

Rolling Stones 'Terrifying'
Atlantic City, EC on 'Little Red Rooster' and 'Boggie Chillum''
(*Japanese triple CD*)

Roger Waters 'Thanks For The Ride'
Stockholm 1984
(*Italian double CD*)

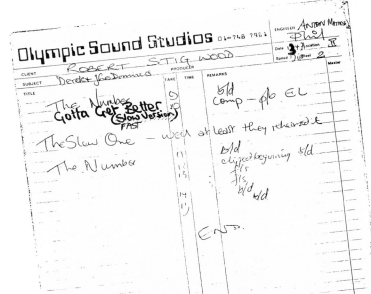

■ G U I T A R / E Q U I P M E N T N O T E S ■

Eric Clapton's first guitar was a £14 acoustic Spanish Hoya. His first electric instrument was a Double Cutaway Kay, which he used in his earliest group The Roosters.

Instruments and amplifiers regularly used at subsequent stages of his career:

Yardbirds
Gibson ES 335
Fender Telecaster
Fender Jazzmaster
Gretsch

Vox AC 30 amp.

Bluesbreakers
Gibson Les Paul
Fender Telecaster

Marshall amp

Cream/
Fender Telecaster

Blind Faith
Gibson ES 335
Gibson Firebird
Epiphone 12 string acoustic
Guild 12 string acoustic

Marshall 100 watt stack
Fender Dual Showman

Plastic Ono Band
Gibson Les Paul
Fender Stratocaster

Fender Dual Showman

Delaney & Bonnie
Gibson Les Paul
Gibson Firebird
Fender Stratocaster

Fender Dual Showman

Derek and the Dominos
Fender Stratocaster

Bangla Desh
Fender Stratocaster
Gibson Byrdland

Fender Dual Showman

Rainbow 'Comeback'
Fender Stratocaster
Gibson Les Paul

Fender Dual Showman

Solo Years: 1974/75
Martin Acoustic
Fender Stratocaster
Fender Telecaster
Gibson Explorer

Music Man amp.

1976
Martin Acoustic
Fender Stratocaster
Fender Telecaster

Music Man amp.

1977
Martin Acoustic
Fender Stratocaster

Music Man amp.

1978–82
Fender Stratocaster

Music Man amp.

1983
Fender Stratocaster
Gibson Explorer
Martin Acoustic

1984
Gibson Les Paul
Fender Stratocaster
Martin Acoustic

Marshall amp.

1985
Fender Stratocaster
Gibson Les Paul
Roland Guitar Synth

Marshall amp.

1986/87
Fender E.C. Signature
Gibson Les Paul
Marshall amp.

1988
Fender E.C. Signature
Gibson Les Paul
Chet Atkins acoustic

Soldano amp.,
Marshall cabinets.

1989–91
Fender E.C. Signature
Chet Atkins acoustic

Soldano amp.,
Marshall cabinets

Music Man discovers MUSIC MAN

INDEX

Page numbers in *italic* refer to the illustrations

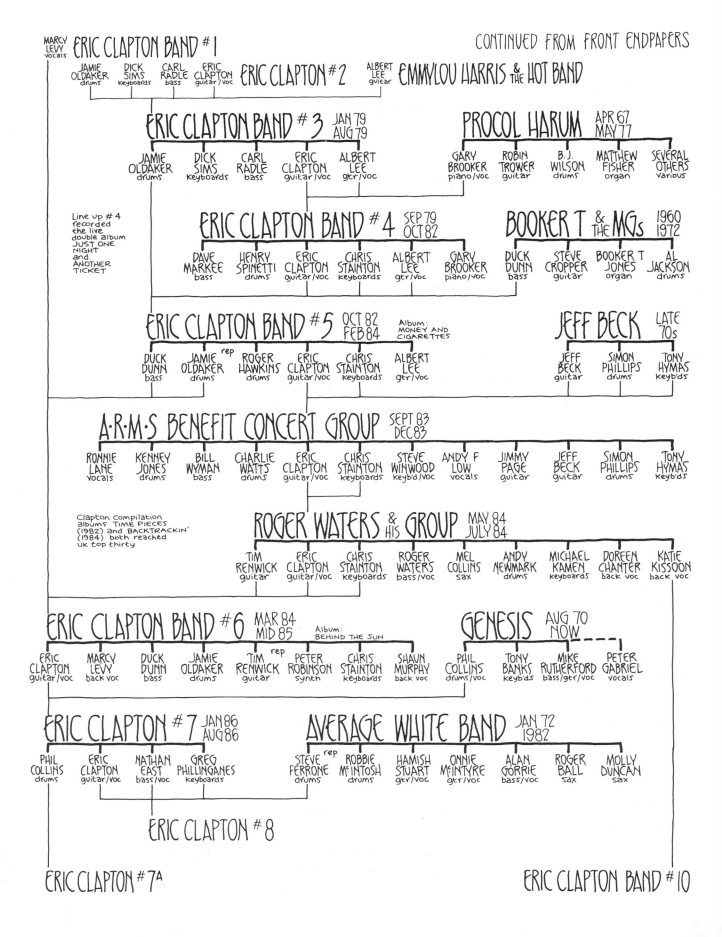

ERIC CLAPTON BAND #1

MARCY LEVY vocals

JAMIE OLDAKER drums

DICK SIMS keyboards

CARL RADLE bass

ERIC CLAPTON guitar/voc

ERIC CLAPTON #2

ALBERT LEE guitar

EMMYLOU HARRIS & THE HOT BAND

ERIC CLAPTON BAND #3   JAN 79 AUG 79

JAMIE OLDAKER drums

DICK SIMS keyboards

CARL RADLE bass

ERIC CLAPTON guitar/voc

ALBERT LEE gtr/voc

PROCOL HARUM   APR 67 MAY 77

GARY BROOKER piano/voc

ROBIN TROWER guitar

B.J. WILSON drums

MATTHEW FISHER organ

SEVERAL OTHERS various

Line up #4 recorded the live double album JUST ONE NIGHT and ANOTHER TICKET

ERIC CLAPTON BAND #4   SEP 79 OCT 82

DAVE MARKEE bass

HENRY SPINETTI drums

ERIC CLAPTON guitar/voc

CHRIS STAINTON keyboards

ALBERT LEE gtr/voc

GARY BROOKER piano/voc

BOOKER T & THE MGs   1960 1972

DUCK DUNN bass

STEVE CROPPER guitar

BOOKER T JONES organ

AL JACKSON drums

ERIC CLAPTON BAND #5   OCT 82 FEB 84

Album: MONEY AND CIGARETTES

DUCK DUNN bass

JAMIE OLDAKER rep drums

ROGER HAWKINS drums

ERIC CLAPTON guitar/voc

CHRIS STAINTON keyboards

ALBERT LEE gtr/voc

JEFF BECK   LATE 70s

JEFF BECK guitar

SIMON PHILLIPS drums

TONY HYMAS keyb'ds

A·R·M·S BENEFIT CONCERT GROUP   SEPT 83 DEC 83

RONNIE LANE vocals

KENNEY JONES drums

BILL WYMAN bass

CHARLIE WATTS drums

ERIC CLAPTON guitar/voc

CHRIS STAINTON keyboards

STEVE WINWOOD keyb'd/voc

ANDY F LOW vocals

JIMMY PAGE guitar

JEFF BECK guitar

SIMON PHILLIPS drums

TONY HYMAS keyb'ds

Clapton compilation albums TIME PIECES (1982) and BACKTRACKIN' (1984) both reached UK top thirty

ROGER WATERS & HIS GROUP   MAY 84 JULY 84

TIM RENWICK guitar

ERIC CLAPTON guitar/voc

CHRIS STAINTON keyboards

ROGER WATERS bass/voc

MEL COLLINS sax

ANDY NEWMARK drums

MICHAEL KAMEN keyboards

DOREEN CHANTER back voc

KATIE KISSOON back voc

ERIC CLAPTON BAND #6   MAR 84 MID 85

Album: BEHIND THE SUN

ERIC CLAPTON guitar/voc

MARCY LEVY back voc

DUCK DUNN bass

JAMIE OLDAKER drums

TIM RENWICK rep guitar

PETER ROBINSON synth

CHRIS STAINTON keyboards

SHAUN MURPHY back voc

GENESIS   AUG 70 NOW

PHIL COLLINS drums/voc

TONY BANKS keyb'ds

MIKE RUTHERFORD bass/gtr/voc

PETER GABRIEL vocals

ERIC CLAPTON #7   JAN 86 AUG 86

PHIL COLLINS drums

ERIC CLAPTON guitar/voc

NATHAN EAST bass/voc

GREG PHILLINGANES keyboards

AVERAGE WHITE BAND   JAN 72 1982

STEVE FERRONE rep drums

ROBBIE McINTOSH drums

HAMISH STUART gtr/voc

ONNIE McINTYRE gtr/voc

ALAN GORRIE bass/voc

ROGER BALL sax

MOLLY DUNCAN sax

ERIC CLAPTON #8

ERIC CLAPTON #7A

ERIC CLAPTON BAND #10